The
Principles
of
Financial
Control
for the new

Millennium

L. C. GREEN, JR.

Published and Distributed by:
Milligan Books
an imprint of
Milligan Books
1425 W. Manchester, Suite B,
Los Angeles, California 90047
(213) 750-3592

First Printing, May 1998
10 9 8 7 6 5 4 3 2 1

ISBN 1-881524-26-4

AUTHOR'S & PUBLISHER'S NOTE
This publication is designed to provide accurate
and authoritative information in regard to the subject
covered. It is sold with the understanding that the
publisher and author is not engaged in rendering
accounting or other professional service. If expert
assistance is required, the service of a competent
professional person should be sought.

For my father who gave me the desire to succeed

For my mother, Ernestine Green, for always saying *you can do it!*

For my wife, Shirley Diane, and my daughter, LaTisha Cheron (L.C. III) for their support, understanding, and encouragement.

I thank all of you for helping me keep money in perspective. Because of all of you, I *know* it's not the most important thing.

Acknowledgment

Thanks to all of my family, clients, and friends who have supported me throughout the years—I could not have done it without you!

Contents

Seventh Principle of Financial Control:

Eighth Principle of Financial Control:

Ninth Principle of Financial Control:

Tenth Principle of Financial Control:

Eleventh Principle of Financial Control:

L. C. Green, Jr. is the founder of Executive Business Service (EBS), a financial management firm. EBS provides both business and financial consulting along with other accounting services. L. C. has been in the accounting and financial management field for more than twenty years.

A Registered Representative with the National Association of Securities Dealers, Inc. (NASD) and a Board Certified Financial Advisor.

Certified by the California State Department of Insurance and Tax Preparer Program, Mr. Green teaches continuing education for insurance and tax professionals.

He has been an Instructor at five colleges in Los Angeles county for over nine years. Mr. Green has taught various subjects: accounting, bookkeeping, taxation, and other related financial management courses.

As a public speaker, he has delivered more than 750 speeches to diverse audiences with emphasis on business and personal financial management.

Mr. Green co-hosts *The Financial Corner* on cable television in the Los Angeles area and is co-producer and CFO of LMBIA Expo & Trade Show held annually.

L. C. Green, Jr. has written numerous articles for various magazines and published several books including:

Steps of Success
The Blueprint to Success in the 1990s
The Stylist's Complete Guide to Success in the 1990s
Bookkeeping–EBS' Easy Method of Learning
Starting and Operating Your Accounting/Bookkeeping Business
Special Report #1040–Understanding Your Taxes

Foreword

It is the first duty of every man not to be poor. George Bernard Shaw

George Bernard Shaw was absolutely right. And the good news is that no one with a steady income needs to be poor. That may sound like a strong statement to those of us who feel poor right this minute. We just need to know what to do with what we have. That's the reason for this book.

Before we get started, let's clear the air surrounding the entire subject of money. First, let's dispel the myth once and for all that money is bad and/or is unimportant. It is not bad and it is definitely important. If individuals do bad things with money, that doesn't make money (in and of itself) bad. We're constantly reminded of its importance whenever we need some. Money is just as important as the food and clothes it buys, the shelter it affords, the education it provides, and the medical bills it pays, and the fun it permits. And that's certain.

Not all the facts of life are about the birds and the bees. Here are a few facts that are seldom reported:

1. At Age 65:

45% of us are dependent on relatives

30% are dependent on charity (not lucky enough to have relatives to help)

23% are still working (because it is <u>necessary</u> to pay the bills)

2% are self-sustaining

Source: Social Security Administration.

Even if these numbers are a little off, these are some troubling statistics indeed.

2. Result of stock trading as an individual (not mutual funds):

97% lose money

2% break even

1% make money

Source: Harvard Business School study.

3. Fewer men are worth $100 at Age 65 than at Age 18.

Assets minus liabilities add up to almost nothing after working for almost 50 years!

Source: Dewey's Economic Tables

4. 85 out of 100 people reaching Age 65 do not have $250.

In the form of ready cash that is not owed to anyone.

Source: Social Security Administration

5. 93% of those who have failed financially said it was because of the lack of a plan.

Ask anyone over Age 65 who's financially insecure and see what they say.

6. Not one person in the United States has deposited money regularly for 20 years.

Delayed spending doesn't count! If you're like almost everyone, when you make deposits, you withdraw the money long before you reach a worthwhile goal (such as retirement).

Source: American Bankers Association

A survey of 450 pension actuaries (people who predict the future) found that no more than 50% of the so-called baby boomers who reach age 65 between 2010 and 2028 will be able, economically, to retire. Four reasons were given:

1. Inadequate contributions to employer pensions.

2. Inadequate personal savings.

3. Too few workers to support Social Security benefits (resulting in inadequate benefits).

4. Escalating and unaffordable health care costs.

The problems most of us have with money begin with not understanding it and how it works. The purpose of this book is to give you an understanding of how money works and how money will work for you.

Please don't let this information discourage you before you begin reading, keep in mind that some of the richest people in the world today were once penniless.

First Principle of Financial Control:

Educate Yourself

There is a void in the education received in this country. Millions of dollars are spent teaching youth and adults to earn money, but we are not taught what to do with the money once it has been earned. So, we must educate ourselves on what to do with our money after earning it.

Smart use of money starts with a plan. For the last several decades, the value of the American dollar has been affected by many factors. The greatest factors are inflation, interest rates, and taxes. These factors, which may fluctuate dramatically, have prompted millions of Americans to plan for their future.

Winning or Losing the Money Game

1. Try to make it fast—a very slight chance of success.
2. Try to make it slowly—a rather good chance of success.
3. Do not try at all (no plan). This choice is the one most people have made and why many have failed in the money game.

According to a survey of financial planners, there are six reasons why most people fail in the drive for financial independence:

1. Procrastination. Time is a tremendous asset and one that is often wasted.
2. Lack of self-discipline. Unable to save part of earnings.
3. Failure to set a financial goal. A well-defined goal and a step-by-step plan are important.
4. Ignorance of what money must do to accomplish a goal.
5. Failure to understand and apply the tax laws.
6. Purchasing the wrong kind of life insurance, securities, or other investments.

Three Sources of Income

1.   Money earned while working.
2.   Money earned at work that is put to work. With proper preparation, one can turn base income into capital. There will come a time when one can change places with this money and let it do the work.
3.   Money received from charity, gifts, bequests, or inheritances.

Three Things To Do With Money

1.   Spend. This eliminates the other two choices.
2.   Lend. Lend/invest in banks, S&Ls, bonds, and government securities. Lending money wisely, with a coordinated plan of the taxability of that money, can make the difference between freedom or financial distress.
3.   Own. Purchase shares of American industry such as mutual funds, stocks, real estate, energy, commodities, precious metals, rare stamps, art objects, antiques, and precious gems. All these items have risk associated with them. Some have very low risk, some have very high risk. However, if you want to enjoy financial independence, we are going to have some risk. When we lend our money to the banks and S&Ls, and insurance companies for a guaranteed interest rate of 2%-7%, it is invested in shares of American industry at 12%-24%. Sometimes the return exceeds 24%. Remember, ownership carries no guarantees.

Educate yourself on the power of compound interest. Learn investment strategies for bonds, stocks, securities, and real estate. Develop a long term relationship with a financial advisor. Read constantly because everything changes rapidly. Ask questions, even those considered silly. We can all benefit from being harder to embarrass. Scam artists greatest ally is our desire to act as though we already know something. That desire often prevents learning. Get the answers needed to make informed decisions. Go to classes and seminars. The bottom line is to take the time to know for yourself instead of relying on "experts." Become an expert on your money. The reality is that no one will ever know your situation as well as you do.

Ask yourself if you're serious about preserving money. If the answer is yes, financial education and training should be an ongoing part of your financial strategy.

Second Principle of Financial Control:

Keep Good Records

Recording daily expenses is a very important principle. A good business records every financial transaction. Every penny coming in and every penny going out is accounted for. In <u>writing</u>. From this raw data, the many reports for management, stockholders, and taxation are assembled. Without the raw data from every financial transaction, and the resulting reports and documents, no business can survive.

You have to be able to count it or measure it if you want to manage it. Doesn't it make sense that the financial principles that are essential for the success and survival of any business are of equal importance in managing the finances of individuals and families???

Recording all expenditures will show how, when, and where the money is going. We will know where we are spending it. We will be able to measure spending performance. In sports, good coaches understand that when performance is measured, performance improves. By measuring our money performance, we improve the way we handle our money. By keeping track of expenses, we will know how much spending we do and still save and invest.

I recently explained this principle of recording expenditures to a friend who decided to look over his bank statement. He found the health club fitness plan he thought he'd canceled two years earlier was still debiting his checking account monthly. For two years he paid for services that were not used. He wasted almost $1,000. Had he been recording his expenditures on a regular basis, this would not have happened.

Another friend found that the bank had not given her credit for a $91 deposit. If she had not started to record her expenditures, she would not have discovered the bank's error.

A client found that she was spending about $150 a month on coffee. She purchased a coffee maker and began making coffee at home. This recaptured $138 per month.

My favorite story is about a client who found that he and his wife had missed $3,000 in tax deductions. This resulted in about $750 in taxes that did *not* have to be paid!

These are just a few examples of savings generated by applying this principle. What most of us don't seem to understand is that progress in our financial lives, not just business, is directly related to our ability to measure—keep records of all expenditures. It will change your life for the better. And that's a certainty. It is one of the few things in life no one ever regrets doing. How many things can we say that about?

If just the *thought* of keeping records causes you to break out in hives, don't despair because you're not alone. Keep it as simple and "non-invasive" as possible. If you carry a planner with you, jot down everything you spend someplace on the daily sheets. Get a cheap old-fashioned steno pad and keep it in a spot (such as the kitchen counter) that you pass every single day. If you have a computer, get a software program such as *Quicken* and let the software do most of the work. It really doesn't matter how or where the records are kept. Just keep them in an orderly, organized manner that can be referred to quickly.

I can practically guarantee that regular recording of expenditures will save you tax dollars. Of course, nothing in life is guaranteed, but I've never known it to fail yet. Daily recording of expenditures, all year, works every time. This is because you will be able to identify and create tax deductions all year long. Recording expenditures all year will not only save tax dollars but will save lots of time and worry at tax time. No more scrambling to prepare to file taxes. That alone is a fabulous incentive to keep good records.

Third Principle of Financial Control:

Set Goals

You must set a goal or life will set one for you. L.C. Green, Jr.

The most powerful force for achieving personal success is goal setting. It is goal setting that can move you from a dream to reality, from wish to fulfillment, from conception to consummation. Goal setting gives concreteness to thoughts and translates thoughts into actions.

Goal setting begins with the ability to dream. Dreams are the vehicle for identifying possibilities. When you dream, you test possibilities against your desires and adopt those that match. Some dreams are like the wisps of clouds that provide momentary interest but bring no rain. Other dreams are substantial, enfolding you like a warm cloak on a cold day. They give you purpose and anticipation of tomorrow.

Your dreams shape your future, determine the height to which you shall rise, and bring you the success you deserve. Your dreams and your ideas for the future are the basis for the goals toward which you will work. What are your dreams? Take time to write them down. Dreams must be captured or they slip through your fingers and disappear into the nebulous realm of "might have been."

All people have dreams but most do not have goals. A dream written down is a goal. A dream not written down is only a wish that will usually slip away.

It is said that only 5% of the people in the world know what they really want to do in life; the rest conceive themselves to be directed by circumstances. Are you going to be in the 5% that chooses to live their lives the way they want to live them? If so, how do you translate your dream into action? The way to get a dream into action is by setting **short, intermediate, and long term goals.**

Goal	When	Total Cost	Amount $ Per Month	Date Completed
Short term (within the year)				
Intermediate (1-5 years)				
Long term (over 5 years)				

Short Term Goals: goals that require **immediate action.**

i.e., I will set up a retirement plan next week and put $200 a month into it. The objectives of short term goals are to help you reach your intermediate and long term goals. They represent your plans for the next few days, weeks, or months.

Intermediate Goals: where you want to be in the next 1-5 years (buying a car might be an example).

Long Term Goals: where you want to be in a year or more.

i.e., I want to retire on an income of $4,500 a month at Age 65.

Use the table above to get started...*now* is a good time to start.

Effective Goal Setting

Goal setting is a process by which uncertainties are controlled and risks are minimized. It is a process by which you decide where you want to go, how fast, how to get there and what to do along the way.

Goals properly set to chart your course must be carefully defined. Proper goals should meet the following criteria. Goals must be:

1. Conceivable
2. Believable
3. Achievable
4. Measurable
5. Controllable
6. Something you really want

Goals demand creativity. They should be shared only with those people who want to see you truly succeed (which is almost NO ONE you know). Goals must be written.

We need written goals in managing money. None of us would build a $500,000 home without a set of plans. What would you think if your building contractor said, "We don't need plans." You'd undoubtedly start looking for another contractor to build your home because you would want to see a plan detailing how your home is going to look.

How different are any of us who are attempting to manage our money without a plan? Think about it, if you earn $40,000 a year for ten years, that amounts to $400,000. Without a plan, most people have only the appreciation in our homes at the end of ten years. And that's if we're lucky enough to own homes that have appreciated. If we want to break this cycle, goal setting is imperative.

Why Set Goals: Good money management begins with goal setting. Goals give you direction and a purpose for the way you spend your money. They motivate and encourage you as you work toward doing things that are important to you. An individual without goals is like a ship without a captain. The ship may have the finest equipment and structure, yet without a captain to steer and chart its course to a designated port, it goes nowhere and may even drift aimlessly onto the rocks.

Goal setting establishes chief aims. It determines purposes. Without such aims, our lives will be like an abandoned ship at sea, tossed by the waves of circumstances, often taking the voyage of least resistance. This may sound trite but it's true. The key is direction and focus. An individual with specific goals is an individual who will display determination and drive. Effectiveness and productivity are greatly multiplied when one has singleness of purpose. Tunnel vision is good when targets are clearly identified.

Goal setting is the initial cause of which success is the final effect.

Goal setting is not a task, but a process, a way of dealing with the world. A number of steps are involved, steps that must be repeated as conditions change.

Step 1

Establish your goals. They must be specific, measurable, time-related, and attainable.

Step 2

Establish priority (from most to least important goals and action steps); identify potential goal conflicts and trade-offs and how they can be resolved.

Step 3

Identify potential problems and obstacles that could prevent you from attaining your goals.

Step 4

Specify the tasks and action steps that must be performed to accomplish your goals.

Step 5

Indicate how you will measure the results you hope to achieve.

Step 6

Establish milestones for reviewing the progress you are making; for example, specific dates on your calendar.

Step 7

Identify the risks that are involved in meeting your goals and what must be done to avoid low chances of success.

Step 8

Identify and seek the help and resources that may be needed to obtain your goals. i.e., professional financial planners, accountants, professional insurance agents.

Step 9

Review progress periodically and revise goals and plans as feedback and results indicate that revision is appropriate.

These are the basic components of effective goal setting. Of course, there are numerous ways of actually going about it. Research and practical experience have shown that these elements are common to almost all successful planning efforts. Become familiar with the process, adapt it to your needs as individually suitable and begin to practice the approach.

Remember, even though there may be things in life more important to you than financial goals: lasting marriages, happy children, fulfilling careers, humanitarian service projects, etc., your ability to function in the important areas of life is greatly influenced by your financial stability. Money matters–good and bad–permeate our entire lives.

Having financial order and control in your life lays a foundation that enables you to devote more time, energy, creativity, and money to family, hobbies, community or humanitarian services.

Financial goal setting is about the love of life: about a better life available to anyone willing to change spending habits in order to achieve worthy financial goals. The amount of time you spend worrying about money is in reverse proportion to how well you manage your money. If you don't like worrying about money, apply the principles in this book. Remember the old adage:

Success happens when preparation meets opportunity.

Planning via goal setting prepares you for opportunity. In setting goals, think about the things that are important to you and your family. The list below can help you decide which things are more important to you than others. Select the things that you and your family feel are most important and place a "1" beside them. Place a "2" beside the things that are somewhat important, and a "3" beside the things that are not very important to you and your family.

As an individual, you may have trouble deciding which item is more important than another. It's even harder when two or more people live together as a family unit and share money. Communicating, compromising, and giving priority to those items that benefit the entire family can help you reach results that are the most satisfying to all family members.

_____religion	_____recreation
_____education	_____family activities
_____save money	_____home furnishings
_____transportation	_____new house
_____start a new business	_____travel
_____pay off debts	_____make lots of money
_____personal appearance	_____other:
_____culture (plays, art, concerts)	_____other:

Once you have decided what is important to you, then you can see the things you want to work toward. For example, if you placed a "1" beside "family activities," your goal may be to go on a family vacation.

You may find it helpful to think first about long-term goals—those you hope to reach in 10 or 20 years or perhaps even longer. Next, decide your goals for the more immediate future -- the next 5 years, for example. Then list your short-term goals for the coming year. This way, your budget includes some savings toward long-term and intermediate goals, and you will not let short-term goals push other goals aside.

Be as specific as possible in setting goals. Your family may decide its long-term goals are a debt-free home, education for children, and savings for retirement. For the coming 5-year period, goals might be buying a car, making a down payment on a home, and buying a washer and dryer. Goals for this year might be reducing debts, establishing an emergency fund, and buying a vacuum cleaner.

As the size, age, and income of the family change, goals change. For example, a young couple works to establish and furnish their home. The family with growing children tries to provide adequate food, clothing, housing, and education with some extras. After children leave home, the parents concentrate on completing financial arrangements for retirement years.

Establish goals that are realistic, measurable, and achievable within a given time period. By following these three criteria, you can make your dreams come true within a specified period of time.

When you have decided your goals, write them down. You will want to refer to them as you develop your spending plan.

Fourth Principle of Financial Control:

Trim Down Spending

That which each of us call our 'necessary expenses' will always
grow to equal our income unless we protest to the contrary.

George Clason

In order for your financial goals to become a reality, you need a plan
to follow in achieving them. And a realistic plan is impossible without understanding the fourth principle of financial control. What and
how you spend is more important than what you earn.

Financial security is more a function of how you spend than how
much money you earn. In reality, we have far more control over what
we spend than what we earn. Another truth is that the lack of money
doesn't cause as much financial stress as does the lack of the ability to
spend our money. The fourth principle is learning to live on less than
you earn so you can have surplus to get out of debt and invest in assets
that appreciate.

The fourth principal doesn't say you have to spend less, just spend
differently. <u>Pay yourself first, not last</u>. We've all heard that since
childhood. Too bad we haven't practiced it since childhood. Don't wait
until the end of the month to see if anything is left over for yourself.
Pay yourself first then make yourself live on what's left for the
remainder of the month. There is no other way.

This principle doesn't sound easy. By now, we all know that much
in life is not easy. No one, regardless of income, can be financially
successful unless they live on less than they earn. The fourth principle

is absolutely essential. Spend less than 100% of your income—put aside some percentage for yourself.

Books usually say save 10%. Not this book. Why? Because most of us don't save anything. How can we be expected to go from saving 0% to 10% overnight? It simply won't happen. Here's what I recommend. If your employer has a 401(k) or other matching savings plan, find out the minimum percentage you can contribute. Start with that amount.

Think about it. If you contribute 2% and your employer adds 1%-2%, a total of 3%-4% will be saved every pay day. Left alone, this will become "real" money in a short time. The best way to do this is to start now. Check with your employer tomorrow and complete the necessary paperwork *tomorrow*, not next week or next month. If your employer does not offer such a plan or if you're self-employed, save 2% of the next check you get. For the time being, let's not worry about the amount of returns in the account, just set it up–*NOW!!*

This principle can be followed if you are over your head in debt. I am following it. I know others who have gotten out of debt and reached their financial goals by following this spending principle. Spend less than you earn. Review principle two (record keeping). You must learn to keep your expenses lower than your earnings.

Work this principle until it becomes a habit. This is a good habit to have—pay yourself first: at least 2% off the top! If you're like most people, you will gradually (or quickly) increase the percentage that you take off the top. One friend of mine started with 6% in 1993 and is currently saving more than 28% of her income every paycheck!! And she says she doesn't even notice the deductions any more. (By the way, she started with 6% because she wanted to get the maximum match from her employer. Her 6% was matched with 4% which means she's been saving at least 10% of her income since 1993.) Not bad for a person who hadn't been saving anything until then. And it can happen to you too.

Don't worry, you'll still be able to pay your debts. If you keep records (Principle #2), you'll soon see where you can trim and easily maintain your standard of living on the percentage leftover after your savings are put away. And **_left alone!_** Leaving the money alone is critical to succeed. I'm not talking about delayed spending. I promise you if you manage to leave it alone for at least six months, the growth will provide the catalyst to permit you to leave it alone. Just six months...not long really. Responsible spending, regardless of your income level, will enable you to get the things you need and want.

The simple truth is that in the absence of a spending plan with clearly defined goals and a method of recording income and expenses, people will spend whatever they earn, sometimes more thanks to easy credit. The person earning $30,000 a year spends it all. The person earning $60,000 a year spends it all. The person earning $80,000 a year spends it all. So don't tell yourself that you'll get started with that next pay increase. *Now* is the right time to start.

As stated, the key to financial security is to live on less than you earn. If the $30,000 per year person forces her/himself to live on $29,000, $28,000, or $27,000, s/he will hardly notice the difference. This is true regardless of your present income $60,000, $80,000, etc. All income brackets will notice amazing changes in their financial problems. Their money worries will disappear because they have money in the bank and the knowledge that they are progressing towards desirable financial goals—getting out of debt, building a retirement, saving for a child's education, etc.

Spend less than you earn—develop this habit. Repeat the following like a mantra until this becomes a habit: *A part of all I earn is mine to keep.*

To help you decide how to "spend and trim," I offer this table:

Guidelines for Spending

Item	Percentage
Housing (include utilities and supplies)	33-35
Food	8-25
Transportation (gas, oil, public transportation)	7-9
Clothing	6-12
Medical (including dental, prescriptions, health insurance)	6-8
Automobile insurance	2-3
Life insurance	2-5
Education	1-2
Credit obligations (include automobile payments)	12-15
Savings	2-10
Recreation/entertainment	2-6
Church/charities	2-6

The above percentages are intended as *guidelines* only, don't get fanatical about the percentages in your spending habits. However, it is very important to reassess in areas that far exceed the percentages in this table. For instance, if you've been spending 15% of your income on clothing, it deserves your attention.

The chart below shows some good guidelines for budgeting.

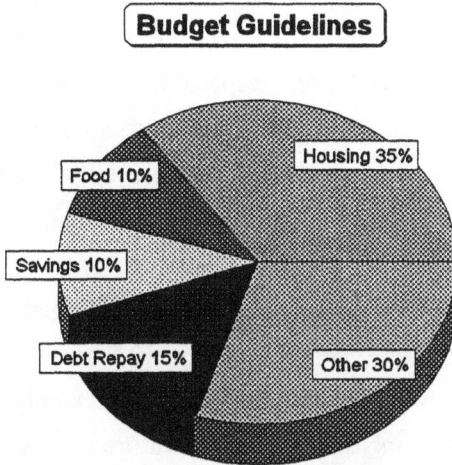

Budget Guidelines

Food 10%

Housing 35%

Savings 10%

Debt Repay 15%

Other 30%

There are detailed worksheets in the Appendixes to help you calculate your expenses and income (see pages 133-138).

Once you have a clear picture of your expenses and income, you can begin to allocate your money. This involves comparing income and expenses, (on a monthly and yearly basis) and reaching a balance that is realistic and workable. If your income is irregular, you must take extra care when you allocate. You will want to set aside enough extra in the months when you have higher income to cover the months when your income is reduced.

When the budget for the year is not in balance, then there is trouble. Three alternatives exist. One is to use savings or borrow money to meet the total budget deficit for the year. This can prevent you from reaching your goals.

A second alternative is to reduce lower priority expense items, or perhaps even cut them out of the budget. This may require sacrifice and the determination and discipline to stick to your decisions.

A third alternative is to increase your income by taking a second job, finding another job that pays more, or adding another earner to the family. This is probably the most difficult alternative as it is likely to result in a significant change in lifestyle. In addition, finding another job may be difficult or even impossible.

Now that you have established between estimated income and expenses, the next step is to develop a spending plan. A spending plan may cover any convenient budget period. However, most plans are for 12 months and coincide with the calendar year (especially true for personal plans).

Using a record keeping book (buy an inexpensive one—plenty available at *Staples, Target,* etc.). Plan your spending by deciding category-by-category how much to spend. For computer buffs, there's excellent software—such as *Quicken*—to help with this. Use the information you recorded earlier to help you decide whether to continue your present pattern of spending or to make changes. If you are satisfied with what your dollars have given your family in the past, allow similar amounts in your estimates of future expenses.

If you are not satisfied with what you got for your money last year or last month, look critically at your spending. Until you study your records, you may be unaware of overspending and poor buying habits. Be realistic in revising your allowances for expenses. The *Budget Guidelines* table and pie chart in this book can help you decide if the revisions are realistic and workable.

Be sure to relate your financial goals listed in the table to your future expenditures. Check to see that future spending plans include those items which you and your family have determined to be important to you.

Write down how much you plan to spend in each category for the budget period, then try to stick to your plan. As purchases are made, write down how much was spent in the appropriate category. At the end of the budget period, total each category. Compare what you spent with what you planned to spend. If your spending was quite different from your plan, find out why so you can improve the next plan.

If your plan did not provide for your family's needs, you will want to revise it. If the plan suited your needs but you had trouble sticking to it, you will want to use stricter self-discipline and better management next time.

A spending plan is something you keep working and reworking until it suits your family and satisfies individual members. Do not expect to have a perfect spending plan the first time you set up one. But with each succeeding budget, you can expect improvement.

Adjust Your Plan to Changes

Although you may be satisfied with your present plan, you need to change it from time to time. As circumstances change, you need to adjust your spending plan according to your new goals, needs, and resources. By thinking through your expenses, setting goals, and keeping records, you are in a better position to make revisions that reflect what is important to you and your family.

There is no magic plan that guarantees financial security. And, because families have different goals, there is no single "right" way to plan. A mistake lots of us make is to try to live with a plan that worked well for someone else. That is seldom a successful approach. There's no way out of doing the work for your personal situation and circumstances. Always remember that what you have in the future depends on what you do with your money today. Sobering thought, isn't it?

Fifth Principle of Financial Control:

Eliminate Debt

Debt is the #1 road block to financial freedom.

One definition of debt: Paying more for goods and services than you need to.

Easy credit began in the early 1960s with no instructions for use. Credit really 'took off' in the 1970s. We worshiped spending in the 1980s. Record bankruptcies in the 1990s have caused us to reconsider the three other decades. The twenty-first century will belong to the saver. This section addresses how to use and control credit.

Recording expenditures, setting goals, and spending differently are key principles in debt management. You may not be able to understand how living on less than 100% of your income can get your debts under control (remember, pay yourself first and live on the rest).

You can start with the way you use credit. You should only use credit cards for emergencies. *Real* emergencies such as car repair on the car you need to get to work and you don't have the cash to pay for the repair. Credit cards should never be used for consumables such as: clothes, food, gasoline, restaurant meals, etc. If you use your credit card for dinner, in twelve hours the food is gone, but at 18%-22% interest, you may pay two-three years to the credit card company. This is very costly!

Let's look at what credit card and other debt can cost you. Start with $650 owed, make minimum payments each month, at 21% interest it will take over 17 years to pay the debt off. And, you will pay about $1,811 in interest. Now, let's take the same example with $10,000. It will take you about 24 years and cost you about $14,500 in interest. Want to figure this out for yourself? If you have access to the World Wide Web, go out to one of these sites:

http://www.interest.com   http://www.financenter.com

To save money, pay with cash. If you don't have the money, don't buy it. Sounds simplistic? Sorry, don't mean to sound caustic or trite, but it eventually gets down to the simple things to get control of your finances. Remember, you can have everything you need but you can't necessarily have everything you want.

(I have learned–the hard way–and I'm trying to point out that anyone can be financially secure on any income if expenses stay lower than earnings.)

Some people have a hard time understanding that stopping credit spending is not the end of spending, just redirecting the way you spend. You become a power spender, realizing the most efficient use of your money in achieving financial goals.

Debt Elimination

There are many ways to eliminate debt. The method recommended here is debt control by the elimination process. Here is how the Debt Eliminator works: Take a sheet of paper and list each outstanding debt, the interest rates charged, the minimum monthly payments, and the remaining balances. On a separate piece of paper, list the debts starting with the one with the lowest balance first.

Pay the minimum payment to all but the smallest debt. Add all available money to the smallest debt until it's paid off (this is often in the first month). When the smallest debt is paid off, pay all available money to the next smallest debt—include the money from the debt you just retired.

The key to making this process work quickly is to keep the dollar amount of the total monthly payment the same until all debt is retired. For example, if the smallest debt is $65 a month and you add $50 to it, your monthly payment will be $115 ($65+$50). When this debt is retired, you add the $115 to the second debt. Let's say the second debt is $125 a month. Your monthly payment is now $240 ($125+115).

When the second debt is retired, you do the same with the third debt and so on. This process will get you out of debt while giving you a feeling of accomplishment as the smallest debts are retired.

The reason for using this process of debt elimination is to get into a situation where you are making double, triple, and quadruple payments as soon as possible. This gives you the feeling you are exterminating your debts with reckless abandon, a wonderful feeling after years of feeling enslaved by them.

Some debt elimination programs advocate eliminating the debts according to the highest interest rate which should result in paying less interest overall. This method does not necessarily result in retiring the greatest number of debts quickly. If your largest debt is also the highest interest, it may take years to retire it and you'll have to continue to make payments to all your other debts in the meantime. I would find this method frustrating. If, however, you'd feel better by paying the least amount of interest overall, by all means, use this alternative method. Both approaches ultimately accomplish the same goal: all debt is retired.

Now, you may be wondering where the additional $50-$100 to quickly eliminate the first debt is coming from. Good question. You'll find it by redirecting your spending and by trimming expenses. It's the unnecessary expenses that will generate the $50-$100 additional per month. Businesses trim expenses all the time to keep profitable. We're all familiar with the notion of downsizing, the 1990s word for firing. Individuals and families should do the same. We need to "fire" those expenses that don't serve our most important goals.

To get more money for something you want, you have to spend less on something else. That's all there is to it. You can speak to the wisest guru in the world and you'll still get the same answer. Everyone finds different ways to save. But here are some suggestions:

★ Bury your credit cards. Charge nothing. Interest payments will then melt away. (Okay, charge something, but not much.)

★ You can lower the price of a round trip air fare by as much as two-thirds by making certain your trip includes a Saturday evening stay over, and by purchasing the ticket in advance. Keep an eye out for fare wars. Be prepared to act quickly. (One more example of why ready cash improves your life. Broke people can't really take advantage of genuine bargains because they have to charge it and pay interest on the "savings.") Visit http://www.priceline.com

★ To make certain you have a cheap fare, even if you use a travel agent, call all the airlines that fly where you want to go and ask what the lowest fare to your destination is.

★ Declare a new-clothes moratorium until you have your present wardrobe paid for.

★ Rental car companies offer various insurance and waiver options. Check with your insurance agent and credit card company in advance to avoid duplicating any coverage you may already have.

★ Rent, don't buy, things you rarely use. Or split the cost with a neighbor (fifty-fifty on the snow blower and all repairs).

★ Buy toilet paper labeled TOILET PAPER. Buy peanut butter labeled PEANUT BUTTER. If you hate the generic stuff, switch back to the higher-priced brand names, but try the cheap one first.

★ You can save thousands of dollars over the lifetime of a car by selecting a model that combines a low purchase price with low financing, insurance, gasoline, maintenance, and repair costs. Ask your local librarian for new car guides that contain this information.

★ Shop with a list and stick to it. No impulse purchases, unless...there's a terrific sale. Then buy by the carton. You say you can't be bothered saving $6.25 on tuna fish in bulk? Do you realize that you need $250 in the bank to earn $6.25?

★ Having selected a new car model, you can save hundreds of dollars by comparison shopping. Call at least five dealers for price quotes and let each know that you are calling others.

★ Use up your savings to get out of debt. Only losers pay 18 percent on their credit cards so they can keep earning 5 percent on their bank accounts.

★ Consider refinancing your mortgage if you can get a rate that is at least one percentage point lower than your existing mortgage rate and plan to keep the new mortgage for several years or more. Ask an accountant to calculate precisely how much your new mortgage (including up front fees) will cost and whether, in the long run, it will cost less than your current mortgage.

★ Before buying any used car: a) Compare the seller's asking price with the average retail price in a "bluebook" or other guide to car prices found at many libraries, banks, and credit unions. b) Have a mechanic you trust check the car, especially if the car is sold "as is."

★ Don't trust any bills, especially those that are computer generated. If you take the time to check for errors, you'll find a lot of overcharges.

★ Refinance any high-rate loan. But use home-equity loans to eliminate credit-card bills only if you're swearing off your credit card. Otherwise, you'll run up your credit card again, winding up with two debts where there used to be one.

★ Consider purchasing a used car from an individual you know and trust. They are more likely than other sellers to charge a lower price and point out any problems with the car.

★ When buying a new home, you can often negotiate a lower sale price by employing a buyer's broker who works for you, not the seller. If the buyer's broker or the broker's firm also lists properties, there may be a conflict of interest, so ask them to tell you if they are showing you a property that they have listed.

★ Do not purchase any house until it has been examined by a home inspector that you selected.

★ Learn to love your neighbors. With them, you can pool services like baby-sitting and transportation. You can even swap skills: You do my taxes, I'll paint your garage.

★ Vacation off-season, when airfares and room rates are cheaper. The sun is just as hot the week before Memorial Day as the week after.

★ When buying major appliances, once you've selected a brand, check the phone book to learn what stores carry this brand, then call at least four of these stores for the prices of specific models. After each store has given you a quote, ask if that's the lowest price they can offer you. This comparison shopping can save you as much as $100 or more.

★ To save as much as hundreds of dollars a year on electricity, make certain that any new appliances you purchase, especially air conditioners and furnaces, are energy-efficient. Information on the energy efficiency of major appliances is found on Energy Guide Labels required by federal law. Check with your electric utility to learn if it has a program to help reduce the costs of any appliance purchases.

★ Sell something that's expensive to keep — for example, a second car that you don't use regularly to drive to work.

★ Don't decide to lease a car just because the payments are lower than on a traditional auto loan. The leasing payments may be lower because you don't own the car at the end of the lease. Leasing a car is very complicated. When shopping, consider the price of the car (known as the capitalized cost), your trade-in allowance, any down payment, monthly payments, various fees (excess mileage, excess "wear and tear," end-of-lease), and the cost of buying the car at the end of the lease.

★ Call your sister in the evening, when rates are lowest. Or don't call. Maybe she'll call you.

★ You can reduce credit card fees, which may add up to more than $100 a year, by getting rid of all but one or two cards, and by avoiding late payment and over-the-credit limit fees.

★ Take a larger deductible on your fire and auto coverage. Cancel collision insurance on an old car. You might find that it's not even worth insuring, because the insurance company won't pay much toward its repair.

★ When buying a new car, you can save as much as hundreds of dollars in finance charges by shopping for the cheapest loan. Contact several banks, your credit union, and the auto manufacturer's own finance company.

★ Look for cheap entertainment. Museums. The zoo. Parks. Walks. Picnics. Parades. Friends.

★ Electricity bills can be reduced by enrolling in load management programs and off-hour rate programs offered by your electric utility company. It may save you up to $100 a year in electricity costs. Call your electric utility for information about these cost-saving programs.

★ You may save tens of thousands of dollars in interest charges by shopping for the shortest-term mortgage you can afford. On a $100,000 fixed-rate loan at 8% annual percentage rate (APR), for example, you will pay $90,000 less in interest on a 15-year mortgage than on a 30-year mortgage.

★ You can save thousands of dollars in interest charges by shopping for the lowest-rate mortgage with the fewest points. On a 15-year, $100,000 fixed-rate mortgage, just lowering the APR from 8.5% to 8.0% can save you more than $5,000 in interest charges. On this mortgage, paying two points instead of three would save you an additional $1,000.

★ If your local newspaper does not periodically run mortgage rate surveys, call at least six lenders for information about their rates (APRs), points, and fees. Then ask an accountant to compute precisely how much each mortgage option will cost and its tax implications.

★ Check with your phone company to see whether a flat rate or measured service plan will save you the most money.

★ Switch to lower-watt bulbs in all but your reading lamps.

★ Shift your credit-card balances to a lower-rate card, then use the interest savings to pay down debt.

★ You will spend less on food if you shop with a list.

★ Pay cash for gasoline instead of using a credit card. You might save up to five cents a gallon at many service stations. And use self-service pumps because they are always cheaper. You can save hundreds of dollars a year by using the lowest-octane called for in your owner's manual. You can save up to $100 a year on gas by keeping your engine tuned and your tires inflated to their proper pressure.

★ Check your local phone bill to see if you have optional services that you don't really need or use. Each option you drop could save you $40 or more each year.

★ Don't just look at the price of the item, you can save hundreds of dollars a year by comparing price-per-ounce or other unit prices on shelf labels. Stock up on those items with low per-unit costs.

★ Clip coupons. There's no point throwing them out with the trash. It's like stepping over money you see on the street. Or going on top of your roof and throwing money off.

★ Consumers lose billions of dollars each year on unneeded or poorly done car repairs. The most important step that you can take to save money on these repairs is to find a skilled, honest mechanic. Before you need repairs, look for a mechanic who: is certified and well established; has done good work for someone you know; and communicates well about repair options and costs.

★ E-mail your friends and your kids instead of calling long distance.

★ Since brand name drugs are usually much more expensive than their generic equivalents, ask your physician and pharmacist for generic drugs whenever appropriate.

★ You can save several hundred dollars a year by purchasing auto insurance from a licensed, low-price insurer. Call your state insurance department for a publication showing typical prices charged by different companies. Then call at least four of the lowest-priced, licensed insurers to learn what they would charge you for the same coverage.

★ Join a home-swap network, for cheaper family vacations.

★ Find new uses for things instead of throwing them out: Start seedlings in the cut-off bottoms of milk cartons. Twist newspapers into cylinders for kindling. The handier you are, the more money you'll save.

★ You can save as much as several hundred dollars each year in lower credit card interest charges by paying off your entire bill each month.

★ If you are unable to pay off a large balance, switch to a credit card with a low annual percentage rate (APR). For a modest fee, Bankcard Holders of America (703-389-5445) and RAM Research Corp. (800-344-7714) will send you a list of low-rate cards.

★ If you want insurance protection only, buy a term life insurance policy. If you want to buy a whole life, universal life, or other cash value policy, plan to hold it for at least 15 years. Canceling these policies after only a few years can more than double your life insurance costs.

★ Have your paycheck directly deposited into your bank because banking institutions often will drop or lower checking fees if paychecks are directly deposited by your employer. Direct deposit offers the additional advantages of convenience, security, and immediate access to your money.

★ If you have a mutual fund, arrange for all dividends to be automatically reinvested. If you keep stocks with a stockbroker, have the payments swept into a money-market fund for reinvestment.

★ Don't spend your next raise. Put the extra money away, even if it's just $20 a week. The more money you earn, the more of it you should set aside. Toward late middle age, you should be saving 15 to 20 percent of your income, at least.

★ Pay off your mortgage faster by doubling up on principal payments every month. You'll build equity sooner, which is a form of saving. You'll also spend much less on interest payments.

★ Quit buying books. Get a library card instead.

★ Don't trade in your car as soon as the loan is paid off. Make repairs, if you have to, and keep it for a year or two longer. Save the money you were spending on monthly car payments.

★ Let the government withhold extra tax money from your paycheck, and save the refund.

The above listed tips are to give you ideas on how to redirect your spending to get out of debt and build a surplus of money for yourself and family. Remember, a successful business always looks at ways to reduce expenses (trimming) to increase profit. Individuals and families must do the same.

Look at debt elimination as a process of preventing future interest payments. If you pay a $650 credit account off in 6-8 months instead of 17 years, you will save $1,100 in interest. A $10,000 credit card debt paid in 5 years instead of 24 years will save about $14,000 in interest. A $100,000 house mortgage paid in 15 years instead of 30 will result in about $92,000 in interest savings. With all these examples, I hope you got my point, paying off debts save you money. Money that can be used for fun instead of increasing the profits of credit card companies.

If your financial problems are such that you can't start to eliminate your debt, you should seek professional credit assistance. Are you in credit trouble?

10 Warning Signs of Credit Trouble

1. Paying only the minimum amount due on your cards.

2. Charging more each month than you make in payments.

3. Using credit and cash advances for items you used to purchase with cash.

4. Having a total credit balance that rarely decreases.

5. Being at or near your credit limit and applying for new cards.

6. Needing a consolidation loan to pay off existing debt.

7. Not knowing the total amount you owe.

8. Feelings of anxiety and stress whenever you use your charge cards.

9. Draining your savings to pay debts.

10. Making bill payments late.

It is to your advantage to eliminate debt as soon as you can because excessive debt problems can even lower your self-esteem. You can call 310-519-9144 for information on Debt Management Services.

The most important thing in controlling debt is not making unnecessary debt because it is the small debts that are beating most people. Five credit cards with minimum payments of $75-$80 a month each total $370 a month. This $370 in a retirement or investment account for twenty years will amaze you. If you just stopped using your credit cards, think of the financial power you would have.

Please remember: It is imperative that you start paying yourself first no matter what your indebtedness. Start saving now. You are not to wait until your debts are paid off before you start. Don't despair, you are going to pay off your debts, you're just going to pay yourself first.

Lazy hands make a man poor, but diligent hands bring wealth.

The above quote is from Proverbs 10:4. This speaks to a universal law that I think applies to finances as well: Whatever you don't use in life, you lose. If you don't consistently use the ability you have to manage your finances properly, eventually that responsibility will be taken away. The opposite is also true. Why do you think the rich get richer? In Matthew 25:14-29 you will find the following story of the talents:

A man, before his journey to another country, called three of his servants together and loaned them money to invest for him while he was gone. He gave ten talents (a unit of currency in those days) to his servants to manage while he was away. He gave five talents to one servant, two talents to another, and one talent to the last–dividing it in proportion to their abilities. He then left for his trip. After a period of time, the master returned from his journey and called upon the servants to account for his money.

The first servant entered with ten talents. He had invested wisely and could return five more than had been entrusted to him. "Good work," his master said. "You are a good and faithful servant. You have been faithful over this small amount, so now I will give you much more."

The second servant entered with four talents. He had invested wisely and could return two more than had been entrusted to him. "Good work," his master said. "You are a good and faithful servant. You have been faithful over this small amount, so now I will give you much more."

The third servant entered with the one talent he had been given and said, "Sir, I knew you were a hard man to please, and I was afraid to lose the only talent you gave me so I buried it and can now return it to you."

The master replied: "You are a wicked and slothful servant! You should have at least made a simple investment so I could have some interest! Take the money from this man and give it to the man with the ten talents. For the man who uses well what he is given shall be given more, and he shall have abundance. But from the man who is unfaithful, even what little responsibility he has shall be taken from him."

The story of the talents is appropriate for us to understand for the following reason: Before significant wealth will come our way and stay we have to master the money already in our control! Begin thinking in terms of handling money the way a good steward would. Pay yourself first!! This cannot be overstated. If you pay yourself last or not at all, you relinquish control of your money and will not be able to save and invest for the future.

Sixth Principle of Financial Control:

Save Money

Saving money is like insurance, you don't realize it's important until you need it. The most common method of saving is making a regular deposit to your savings account. Another method is to save by payroll deduction–the employer deducts a fixed amount from the employee's paycheck each pay period and applies it to a designated savings vehicle. This is a popular and easier method because it gets the money out of your hands before you can spend it.

If your employer doesn't have a payroll deduction plan, many banks will debit your checking account each month and deposit it in a savings account. But, if you want to write a check to deposit in your savings account, make sure it is the first check you write when you sit down to pay your bills. It may be difficult but the saving habit is its own reward.

Saving money consistently will prepare you for investing. And a cash reserve is usually considered the foundation of any financial plan. The main benefit of your cash reserve is that you earn a safe and guaranteed return and the funds can be converted to cash without a penalty or loss of principal. Having a large cash reserve to cover several months of living expenses is indeed a worthwhile goal, but let's not try to do too many things at once. Since we are not a nation of savers, let's just save consistently first. Frankly, the intended use of the savings is a personal decision.

A cash reserve deserves your consideration because it gives you an immediate supply of hard cash to cover monthly expenses in the event of an emergency. Creating a cash reserve will take some discipline, but it is the foundation of your investment program and will protect you from financial hardship.

But where do you get the money to save? Here are some more ideas:

Pay Yourself First

Yeah, yeah, yeah, I know I've said this before. I'm deliberately repeating myself because most folks make tens of thousands of dollars over the course of a year. The vast majority of it goes to pay someone or something else: local, state, and federal taxes, the mortgage or rent payment, car loan or lease, the supermarket, etc. Shouldn't you also pay yourself at least a few pennies out of each dollar you earn?

The surest way to make sure you get a slice of your own income is to have money deducted from your pay before you have a chance to spend it. The best options for saving through payroll deduction are employer-sponsored plans, such as 401(k) or 403(b)(7) retirement programs, that provide tax savings and, often, matching contributions from the employer. In essence, you get a tax deduction for the amount you save, your investment earnings pile up on a tax-deferred basis, and you may get some extra money thrown in. Simply put, there's no better way to accumulate wealth.

If your employer doesn't sponsor such a plan, you may be able to save automatically in other ways. Perhaps part of your paycheck can be deducted for deposit into a credit union account or to purchase U.S. Savings Bonds. Or you might use automatic investing programs to make regular investments from your bank checking or savings account into a mutual fund or other investment vehicle. Automatic investing provides the discipline that everyone requires in order to put money aside for important goals such as retirement, college, or buying a home.

Also, by investing regularly, you are employing a proven investment technique: Dollar-cost averaging.

Save That Raise

Another proven technique is to make certain you save at least part of any raise you get. If you were able to get by before you got the raise, you should be able to save at least half of it. The key, once again, is to start saving the extra money before you get accustomed to spending it. You may be able to boost the percentage of your pay that goes into your employer-sponsored savings plan or increase the dollar amount of an automatic investing arrangement.

Suppose, for example, that a 35-year-old increases her savings by $40 a week. Assuming an average annual total return of 7%, the $40-a-week investment will be worth more than $100,000 by the time she reaches the age of 65.

Don't Let Windfalls Blow Away

Try to save a substantial portion–at least half–of any unexpected cash you receive. Such "windfalls" as tax refunds, birthday gifts, or overtime earnings can add a powerful boost to your savings and investment program. If you stash the cash into your mutual fund or bank savings account before you get tempted to spend it, you can take advantage of the power of compounding to accumulate money toward important goals.

Make Loan Payments To Yourself

Don't get rattled, I'm not talking about what may have come to your mind. When you've paid off a car loan, credit-card balance, or college loan, keep on making the payments–to yourself. If you're accustomed to paying $200 a month toward a loan, you should be able to keep writing a $200 check to your mutual fund or savings account each month. For most American consumers, car payments are the second biggest regular expense, after housing. If you can keep that car running for a while after paying it off, you can pile up impressive amounts.

Then, next time you have to buy a car, you may be able to make a bigger down payment and shorten your payment schedule. Keep up this discipline and eventually you may build up enough savings to pay cash for your cars, avoiding costly finance charges completely. Heck of a thought, isn't it? Imagine the look on the face of the car salesperson!

Making Pennies Count

Some super savers make a game of finding ways to increase the amount they put away. Among their winning moves:

★ If you get paid every two weeks, keep to a budget based on two paychecks a month. But in two months of each year, you'll get a third paycheck. Try to save the bulk of those "extra" paychecks.

★ Pay a few bucks extra toward credit-card balances so you pay them off earlier. Concentrate on the highest-cost card first, then work to pay off the next.

★ Stash your change in a jar. But don't let the coins sit there forever. When you've accumulated $100 or so, add it to your savings. If you add an average of 50 cents a day to your change jar, you'll be able to save nearly $200 a year.

★ Unless it's a true necessity, avoid buying an item on credit. Instead, save up until you can buy that new piece of clothing, electronic gadget, or weekend getaway trip. You'll avoid paying interest. As a bonus, you may find that you'll avoid some impulse purchases.

★ Speaking of impulse buys, try waiting 24 hours before purchasing any item that is not a necessity. You may find that the urge can be resisted if you wait a day.

★ When you write a check, round up the amount you subtract to the next highest dollar. If your check is for $24.50, deduct $25 from your balance. Over time, you'll build up the amount in your account. Once or twice a year, you can put the excess that you've accumulated through this trick into your savings or mutual fund account.

Our habits determine "who" and "what" we are. Saving money is a good habit. The best part is that once you start a regular savings and investment program, you may be surprised at how even modest amounts can grow over the course of a couple of years. "Slow but steady" was a winning strategy for the fabled tortoise. It is also a winning formula for financial success.

Seventh Principle of Financial Control:

Invest Money

How much risk is right for you? This is the first step before you invest *any* money anywhere! How much risk you can afford depends on four factors:

Your Stage of Life

The needs and demands on your income differ depending on whether you're just starting out, raising a growing family, putting children through college, in your prime earning years or getting ready for retirement.

Your Income

People with lots of discretionary income can afford to take greater risks with their money than people who are just getting by or who depend on their investments for their income.

Your Assets

The more assets you currently have, the more risk you can probably afford to take.

Your Attitude

Some people are comfortable with high levels of risk. Others aren't. Don't do anything _you_ are not comfortable with.

There is a difference between an investor and a saver. An investor puts his money at risk in order to achieve a higher financial return. The saver is one who tries to preserve and keep his money safe. The saver is more concerned with getting his original investment back. He looks for financial vehicles that are safe and guaranteed.

An investor commits money where the return is not guaranteed. Sometimes the investment is not safe. When the investment is sold, he may receive more or less than he put in. The investor realizes that what he gives up in safety, he may get back many times in higher returns. It is best to have a certain amount of money saved and a separate amount to invest.

The key to building wealth begins with an investment fund. Once you have enough money in your cash reserve fund, you can start your investment fund. The money for your investment fund will come from your regular savings pledge and any excess you have accumulated in your cash reserve fund.

The goal for your investment fund will be to earn higher yields than could be earned in a regular savings account. In exchange for a higher yield, you must be willing to accept a slightly higher degree of risk.

There are two general categories of money invested, for income and for appreciation. Income investments are usually placed in different types of bonds and select stocks. Appreciation or growth investments include growth stocks and real estate.

The return on your investment should outweigh the risk. The relationship between risk and return does not mean that you will always earn higher returns on your investment by taking greater risk. But, if there is a higher degree of risk, you should expect a higher return.

Diversification is a key element to sensible investing. Like your grandmother said: "Don't put all your eggs in one basket." Diversifying your investments spreads out the inherent risk. A good investment today may not be good next month or next year. It is wise to purchase several investments that together will meet your needs and out-perform the average. This way, you spread out and (usually) reduce the risk.

When it comes to investments, risk is related to reward. The general rule is the greater the risk, the higher the reward. But you can't assume this will always be true. A poor quality investment is a poor quality investment, period. When considering risk, here are some factors to consider:

Expected Return: It's impossible to gauge exactly how much an investment will actually return to you. Almost every prospectus, in fact, contains a statement something like "past performance is no guarantee of future success." But on the whole, unless something major changes, such as a change in a mutual fund's manager or a fire in a plant, an investment's returns averaged over several previous years will give you some idea how the investment will do in the future.

Volatility: The value of stocks and bonds fluctuates, depending on the market and the individual investment. It is measured by the volatility index. The volatility index indicates how much a stock or bond's value varies from its average price. It is quoted in + or - dollars. An investment with high volatility is a riskier investment.

Real Return: Inflation has a big impact on investments. During the 1970's, for example, bond and CD interest rates were very high. But the country was also suffering under double digit inflation. To determine the real return, subtract the inflation rate from your gross return. So the real return on a 16% CD during a 12% inflation period would be only 4%.

Types Of Investments

Basically there are four different types of investments:

<u>Real Estate</u>: If you own your home, you are an investor. In fact, your home is probably the biggest single investment you'll ever make. Historically, real estate always appreciates in value. How fast depends on the local market. But when you sell your home, you can usually expect to make a profit. (See Appendix for home buying hints.)

Bonds: Bonds are debt obligations issued by corporations and governments. They are for a fixed sum and pay interest. They have a maturity date, the date when the issuer must pay back the loan. Bonds carry a burden of risk of default and are rated for their safety by two organizations: Standard & Poors and Moody. S&P rates bonds from AAA to D, with AAA being the safest. Moody rates bonds from Aaa to C, with Aaa being the safest.

Government bonds include Treasury Bills, T-Notes and Treasury Bonds, obligations issued by federal government agencies such as Fannie Mae, Ginnie Mae and Sallie Mae, and savings bonds. In addition, state and local municipalities issue tax-free bonds. Corporate bonds are issued by businesses. There are also bond mutual funds.

Stocks: When you buy a stock, you buy a portion of a corporation. A business, when it incorporates, authorizes a certain number of shares of the corporation. Each share represents an equal portion of ownership in the corporation. Shares of brand new corporations have a par value- the value printed on the face of the stock certificate- but that number quickly becomes irrelevant. What is relevant is how much investors are willing to pay for the share. That is its selling price and represents the market value of the share. In addition, a share has a book value. The book value is the value of the assets of the corporation, should the corporation be dissolved and the assets sold off.

Futures, Options And Commodities: These are all highly risky investments in which you guess or speculate at the future prices. They are not for the average investor.

All investments involve some degree of risk, here are some ideas and solutions that reduce risk.

Annuities
Annuities are insurance contracts designed as retirement plans that are a cross between a CD and a non-deductible IRA. Since annuities are

only offered by insurance companies, this information could have been placed in the chapter on insurance. Annuities are covered here because they more closely resemble investments than insurance protection.

An annuity is actually the opposite of life insurance. Life insurance is the systematic accumulation of an estate for protection against financial loss resulting from premature death. In contrast, an annuity is the systematic liquidation of an estate in such a way that it provides protection against the economic difficulties that could result from outliving personal financial resources. The period during which premiums are paid for the purchase of an annuity is called the Accumulation Period. The period during which annuity payments are made is called the Annuitization Period.

During the Accumulation Period, earnings grow tax-deferred. Once the Annuitization Period begins, the recipient (annuitant) receives periodic payments which consist of both principal and interest. Whether the entire payment or only the interest is taxable depends upon the type of annuity plan.

Annuities may also use a beneficiary designation. However, the use of one is limited to either death of the annuitant prior to annuitization or the portion of the principal and interest that has not been returned to the annuitant prior to death.

In most cases there is a surrender charge and penalty charge should an annuitant make a withdrawal prior to age 59½.

Type of Annuities

- **Single Premium Immediate Annuity** (SPIA) A single premium, sometimes called lump sum, is paid into an account from which the annuitant will begin to draw the periodic benefits.
- **Single Premium Deferred Annuity** (SPDA) A single premium is paid into an account in which the annuitant will draw the periodic benefits from some specified point in the future.

- **Flexible Premium Deferred Annuity (FPDA)** Flexible contributions may be made as often and in whatever amounts the contract owner desires (most insurance companies set minimum amounts).

- **Variable Annuity** A variable annuity bundles a collection of mutual funds into a tax deferred wrapper. Contract owner can switch money between funds without triggering taxes, and earnings grow tax deferred until withdrawal. The insurance component of the investment is a guaranteed death benefit. The insurance benefit is a guarantee to pay the value of the retirement account either at death or when the payment period starts, whichever is sooner. Most contracts pay at least the principal amount the customer contributed over the years, even if the stock market wipes out the account entirely.

Balanced Portfolio

The best way to reduce your risk is with a balanced portfolio. Rather than placing "all of your eggs in one basket," diversify your investments. The key to a balanced portfolio is acquiring the right combination of assets. This is where a professional financial planner can help.

Long-Term Investing

Another way to reduce risk is to invest for the long term. Historically, the market has always risen, despite day to day fluctuations and periodic "corrections." Investing for the long term lets you take the slightly higher risks you need to beat inflation and earn a higher return.

Dollar-Cost Averaging

With Dollar-Cost Averaging, you invest exactly the same amount every week, month, quarter or year, regardless of the market. This gets you into the investment habit. You build your investment steadily, without putting too much or too little at the wrong time. Because the market has grown approximately 10% annually, this type of investing averages out the highs and lows of the market and you usually end up paying less per share.

Buy Low. Sell High

"Buy low. Sell high" is one of the oldest maxims of investing in stocks. But it's impossible to determine exactly the right time to buy or sell.

The best way to gauge a stock's or mutual fund's performance is to compare it to a benchmark. For the whole market, the two indexes most investors use are the Dow Jones Industrial Average ("the Dow") or Standard & Poor's 500 Stock Index ("the S&P 500"). The various industries and market segments also have their own indexes. Now for a little basic information.

What is stock?

A share of stock represents ownership in a corporation. A corporation is owned by its stockholders—often thousands of people and institutions—each owning a fraction of the corporation.

When you buy stock in a corporation, you become a part owner or stockholder. You immediately own a part, no matter how small, of every building, piece of office furniture, machinery—whatever the company owns.

As a shareholder, you stand to profit when the company profits. You are also legally entitled to a say in major policy decisions, such as whether to issue additional stock, sell the company to outside buyers, or change the board of directors.

Corporations can issue two type of stock: common and preferred. Each type of stock has its own characteristics and trades independently of the other in the marketplace.

A corporation issues common stock first. It represents the basic ownership of a corporation. Owners of common stock share directly in the success or failure of the business. If the company prospers, common stock owners can benefit through dividend increases and higher stock prices. In return for the ability to participate in higher profit, however, common stock owners take a back seat to preferred stockholders when it comes to distribution of dividends.

Common stock offers you the best possibility of growth, and is considered by most experts to be a hedge against inflation. Investing in common stocks offer you an excellent opportunity to participate in the growth of a company and the nation's economy, but is riskier than investing in preferred stocks or bonds.

A corporation only issues preferred stocks after common stock has been issued. Many investors seem to feel that "preferred" means better. The word preferred relates to preferential treatment over common stockholders when it comes to the distribution of dividends. And, should the company be forced to go out of business and sell its assets—a process called liquidation—preferred stockholders are entitled to receive the money they've invested before common stockholders receive theirs. In exchange for these benefits, preferred stockholders must accept a fixed dividend payment, regardless of any increase in company profits.

Although the economic outlook may seem uncertain, based on history, the potential for above-average returns is still in the stock market.

How do investors actually make money in stock? As a rule, the better a company does and the higher its profits, the more money its stockholders make. Investors buy stock to make money in one or both of two ways:

1. Through dividend payments while they own stock.

2. By selling the stock for more than they paid.

Many companies parcel out portions of their annual profits to stockholders in the form of quarterly dividend payments. Dividend payments vary from stock to stock. Stocks with consistent histories of paying high dividends are known as income stocks because investors often buy these stocks for the current dividends rather than for the company's future prospects.

Some companies, however, reinvest most of their profits back into the business in order to expand and strengthen it. As a result, companies that pay little or no dividends are called growth stocks because investors expect the company to grow and the stock price to grow with it. The average investor does not have the time, expertise, or inclination to buy stock of individual companies unless they are part of a mutual fund.

What are bonds?

When a governmental body or agency or a corporation wants to raise money, one way they can do it is to float a bond issue. When you buy a bond, you are essentially loaning money to the issuer. You expect to earn interest and to be repaid your principle on the maturity date (the date when the bond must be repaid).

Bonds are not without risk. Bond prices go down when interest rates go up. If you have to sell your bond before maturity and interest rates have gone up, the bond will be worth less than its face value. You'll lose money with the sale.

In addition, you face the risk that the borrower may default on repayment of your capital. To help bond investors determine this kind of risk, both Standard & Poors and Moody's have developed ratings for bonds. S&P rates bonds AAA to D, with AAA being the safest. Moody's ratings range from Aaa to C, with Aaa being the safest. To protect your investment, you should buy only AAA, AA or Aaa rated bonds.

Bonds deserve consideration for another reason. For the past decade the stock market has been extremely strong that many investors have ignored the weaker bond market. The bond market does offer one advantage that the stock market does not. Many government issues are tax-exempt. That means not only do you earn interest, but you do not pay taxes on the interest you earn. That can amount to an extra 15% to 31% in your pocket, depending on your tax bracket.

Better yet, let experts do the work and buy Bond Mutual Funds. One of the ways of protecting yourself against risk when investing in bonds is to use bond mutual funds. Like stock mutual funds, bond mutual funds offer the advantages of diversification, professional management and convenience. They also allow you to enter the bond market with a small amount of capital.

What are mutual funds?

A mutual fund is a collection of stocks, bonds, and other securities purchased by a group of investors and managed by a professional investment company. Investing in mutual funds can be a safe and convenient way to invest in stocks or bonds. Basically, here's how a mutual fund works:

The money you invest in a mutual fund is pooled with other investors money. When you invest, you buy shares in a particular fund, not the mutual fund company itself. The aggregate money invested in the fund is then used to trade in a variety of stocks, bonds, or a combination of both. Each mutual fund you own represents participation in all the companies, governments, etc.

As a shareholder, you own a proportionate share of the fund. Each share represents ownership in all the fund's underlying securities. Funds pay dividends and capital gains in proportion to the number of fund shares owned. Thus, if you invest $1,000 you'll get the same rate of return as if you invest $10,000.

Mutual funds can make money for you in two ways. One, they can pay dividends earned from the funds' investments. And two, if a security held by a fund is sold at a profit, the fund can pay capital gains. A Mutual fund company pools your money with money from other people who have similar investment objectives. Mutual funds have many benefits:

Diversification

Remember my advice about not putting all your eggs in one basket? Well, mutual funds–by their very nature–prevent you from doing that. Your best protection against risk is diversification because your investment is spread across dozens of securities instead of just one. Mutual funds provide an assortment of investment options. They offer growth, income, or both, and the opportunity to invest in international markets, as well as the United States. A fund's portfolio managers typically invest in as many as 50 to 200 or more different securities. In effect, they put your money in many baskets instead of just one. Only the most affluent investors can attain the diversification on their own that mutual funds can for their shareholders.

Professional Management

With mutual funds, you have built-in professional money managers who base their buying and selling decisions on extensive, ongoing economic research. After analyzing stock market conditions, interest rates, inflation and the financial performances of individual companies, these managers select investments that best match the fund's objectives. Professional money management has long been available to large institutions and wealthy investors. Mutual funds make this type of financial expertise accessible to everyone. Mutual funds offer many favorable attributes, among them:

Growth

Mutual funds create the possibility of higher long-term returns than conventional savings. According to the Investment Company Institute, as of 12/31/95, mutual funds managed more than 131.8 million shareholder accounts valued over $3 trillion. They have become the nation's third largest financial intermediary—behind commercial banks and life insurance companies.

One reason for mutual fund growth is their performance record in relation to what individuals might expect by investing on their own. Of course, performance varies from fund to fund, but on average and over the long run, the growth of stock funds has paralleled the growth in the U.S. economy. Additionally, bond and money market funds have reflected the long-term movements in their respective markets.

Convenience

Mutual funds are easy to buy. For example, you can purchase funds through a professional investment representative who can help you analyze your financial needs and objectives and recommend appropriate funds. You can get your investment program started for as little as $100. Subsequent investments can be made for as little as $25.

You also have easy access to your money, making your investment a liquid asset. You can redeem all or part of your shares any day the New York Stock Exchange is open and receive the current value of the investment, which may be more or less than the original cost. Payment for redeemed shares will generally be made within three days. (These terms are spelled out in the fund prospectus.)

Flexibility

Mutual funds offer various features that allow you to stay in control of your investments.

Automatic Reinvestment of Dividends and/or Capital Gains

Most mutual funds allow you to automatically reinvest your dividends and capital gains in the purchase of additional fund shares at no extra cost. Over time, the power of compounding can significantly increase the value of your assets.

Exchange Privilege

Within a fund family, you can generally exchange portions of your investment into other funds with different objectives as your financial situation changes.

Before investing, educate (Principle #1) yourself on the types of mutual funds. There are many types of mutual funds and proper research should be conducted prior to purchasing a specific fund! (If you start with your employer's 401(k) plan—always the place to start if your employer matches—the fund family will be determined by your employer. You will still need to know which type of funds to choose.) Here's a brief rundown of the type of funds.

First of all, understand that a mutual fund is not risky or conservative, it's what the fund invests in that determines its level of risk.

Aggressive growth funds seek maximum capital gains as their investment objective. These funds may invest in stocks that are somewhat out of the mainstream—such as smaller-, lesser-known companies that managers believe possess dynamic potential. Current income isn't a significant factor for shareholders in these funds.

Growth funds typically invest in stocks and seek capital growth through the price appreciation of the securities held in their portfolio. Their primary aim is to produce an increase in the value of their investments rather than a flow of dividends.

Growth and income funds invest primarily in the common stock of companies with longer track records. These funds have the expectation of a higher share value but also maintain a solid record of paying dividends.

Balanced funds invest in both stocks and bonds. They emphasize the growth potential of stocks as well as the relative stability of income from bonds.

Income funds seek a high level of current income, which is often achieved by investing in the common stock of companies with good dividend-paying records. They may invest in such fixed-income securities as corporate and government bonds. Some income funds maintain more aggressive objectives than others: High-yield corporate bonds have potential to produce greater income than government bonds. In turn, government bonds are considered less volatile than high-yield bonds. Higher-yielding bonds have a greater risk of price fluctuation and loss of principal and income than U.S. Government Securities, which guarantee repayment of principal and interest if held to maturity. *Municipal bond* funds invest in bonds issued by local governments—such as cities and states—which use the money to build public entities such as schools. Income earned from these securities is usually federally tax-exempt for most shareholders.

Money market funds participate in short-term investment instruments that are considered the safest, most stable type of securities available. By investing in such funds, shareholders can earn current money market interest rates and maintain asset liquidity. In addition, these funds may specialize by investing in tax-exempt money market securities.

Another type of mutual fund worth considering is an **Index** fund. An index measures the ups and downs of a particular type of investment. A good example is the Standard and Poor's 500-stock index (S&P 500). This index gives you the daily average price of the stock of 500 leading companies. There are also indexes that track the performance of bonds, smaller-company stocks, and international stocks. An index mutual fund owns all of the stocks (or a representative number of stocks) in a particular index. So it copies the way that market performs. If the S&P 500 goes up 5 percent, and you have an S&P index fund, you should gain 5 percent minus the fund's expenses.

Most mutual funds are always trying to beat the index, but they rarely succeed. A fund that is hot one year may be cold the next. The beauty of an index fund is that it always does better than the average fund in its group.

Picking an Index Fund

Since index funds are virtually all alike, you want the one with the lowest fees. The less a fund charges you for money management, the better the returns you're going to get. You pay the least for the index funds managed by the Vanguard Group in Valley Forge, Pennsylvania (800-523-2566). There's no sales charge up front and no fee when you sell. The annual management fee for Vanguard's S&P 500 fund is only 0.19 percent a year — on a $3,000 investment, that's a mere $5.70. Vanguard's minimum investment if you don't qualify for an Individual Retirement Account is $3,000. If you buy it for an IRA, you can start with as little as $1,000. Vanguard also has index funds for smaller-company stocks, international stocks, and U.S. bonds.

Some other companies have index funds too. Dean Witter and Schwab offer them for as little as $1,000. Be sure to compare their costs (including exit fees) to Vanguard because they may be higher.

If you won't touch your mutual fund investment for many, many years, nothing beats buying stock-owning mutual funds. Occasionally prices will drop, but they have always gone back up.

In real life, however, you might have to tap your investment earlier than you thought. To avoid the risk of having to sell stocks when they're down, include a bond fund in your investment program. If you have to raise cash, you can usually sell the bond fund without taking a major loss.

Each of the following stock/bond combinations roughly matches one of Vanguard's LIFEStrategy index funds.

Married, no children: Vanguard's *Growth Portfolio*—65% U.S. stocks, 15% foreign stocks, 20% bonds.

Married with children: *Moderate Growth Portfolio*—50% U.S. stocks, 10% foreign stocks, 40% bonds.

Divorced with children and young retirees: *Conservative Growth Portfolio*—35% U.S. stocks, 5% foreign, 40% bonds, 20% short-term investments (similar to cash).

Retirees around 75 and up: *Income Portfolio*—20% U.S. stocks, 60% bonds, 20% short-term.

You don't have $1,000 to get started with the Vanguard Group? No problem. Pioneer Fund of Boston lets you enter for as little as $50. Pioneer started in 1928 and reports that it has never had a losing year. They paid their shareholders even during the Great Depression of the 1930s. They can be reached at 800-225-6292.

Vanguard and Pioneer are mentioned here to give you a place to start if you want to proceed on your own. Please do not construe this as investment advice! Investment decisions should be made carefully after reviewing prospectuses. The best approach is to partner with a financial planner or consultant who can provide up-to-date information regarding specific mutual funds.

Keep in mind....Mutual fund performance will vary. An investor's shares, when redeemed, may be worth more or *less* than original cost.

Tips On Building Your Portfolio
Making your portfolio grow is the goal of every investor. Here are some useful tips to help you increase your investment portfolio.

Tip 1: Have a plan.

Tip 2: Have goals.

Tip 3: Do your homework. Read prospectuses, check indexes, find out all you can.

Tip 4: Invest regularly.

Tip 5: Reinvest your proceeds.

Tip 6: Diversify.

Tip 7: Stick to mainstream investments.

Tip 8: Pick quality investments such as high grade bonds, stocks and securities with a strong track record.

Tip 9: For growth, focus on stocks. Invest for the long term.

Tip 10: Avoid commodities, options and futures.

Tip 11: Avoid limited partnerships.

Tip 12: Remember to figure the actual return-the expected return minus inflation.

Tip 13: Monitor your investments periodically. Check your investments' returns against their benchmarks.

Tip 14: Don't panic and sell a good investment when it's in a slump.

Tip 15: Don't get greedy and hang onto an investment you were planning to sell at a certain price because you think it might go higher.

Tip 16: Never give a broker the right to buy or sell without your prior approval.

Tip 17: Never buy from a stranger over the phone.

What Can A Financial Planner Do For You?

There's an old saying that "if you don't know where you're going, you'll never get there." No where is that more true than with investing. Even if you're just starting out, you can profit from a financial planner. Here's what one can do for you.

Help You Define Your Goals. There is more to setting goals than just saying, "I'd like to have enough to retire on. "A financial planner can help you pin point where you are right now and where you'd like to be. He or she can also help you identify what other factors you'll have to take into consideration. These can be things like needing to pay for a child's college education or an elderly parent's care. A financial planner can help you decide exactly how much you'll need to have put away to meet your goals.

Help You Set An Investment Strategy. A financial planner looks at where you are right now... your current situation, your current income, your assets and the demands on your income, and your attitude toward risk to help you decide how much risk you can afford to take. He then helps you create a financial plan or investment strategy that details how to allocate your investment capital.

Help You Choose Individual Investments. Once you have created your investment strategy, a financial planner can help you identify the places to put your money. A financial advisor spends most of the time tracking these markets and the behavior of individual mutual funds, stocks, bonds and other investments. Financial planners can tell you which investment instruments might best help you reach your goals.

Remember, whether you rely on your own knowledge and intuition or someone else's, there are no guarantees. No financial planner is right all of the time. But a financial advisor is a professional, and you can benefit from the financial planner's knowledge and experience.

Tips On Selecting A Professional Financial Planner

Tip 1: Ask questions. You have a right to know how your money will be invested and how your financial planner does business.

Tip 2: Learn how the financial planner will be compensated. Financial planners are paid either a commission or a portion of the portfolio's value or a portion of the profits. Of the three, receiving a percentage of the profits puts the greatest pressure on financial planners to perform well. Receiving a portion of the portfolio's value puts some pressure on the financial planners to perform, since financial planners can increase their income by increasing your   assets. Receiving a commission on each sale puts no pressure on the advisor at all.

Tip 3: Find out the financial planner's credentials. Unfortunately, in the United States, anyone can call themselves a financial planner or a financial advisor. As a result, many investment sales people use this term without having the training to back their claim. You have the right to know what kind of training your financial planner has. If the answers to your questions are vague or equivocal, be suspicious. Financial planning takes knowledge! Don't settle for anything less than the equivalent of a college degree.

Tip 4: Investigate the financial planner's track record. If the advisor does well for others, he or she will probably do well for you. Ask questions. Find out what "well" means to that advisor. Ask to see numbers. After all, it's your money.

Tip 5: Get references. The best way to find a good financial advisor is to be referred by a friend or acquaintance whose own portfolio has grown thanks to the advisor. Short of that, ask the advisor for references and check them out carefully.

Tip 6: Don't buy from someone who calls you cold on the phone. Be careful! There are a lot of scams out there and it's hard to track down someone who has bilked you over the phone. A reputable investment planner does business face to face and has a real office. Remember, if it sounds too good to be true, it probably is.

Protect Yourself, Loved Ones, & Assets

I'm talking about the dreaded "i" word: Insurance! One of the most misunderstood and poorly understood words in American language. More of us have wasted money in this area than in any other. I will attempt to explain the concept of insurance, and explain the different types so you can decide for yourself what's best for your situation and circumstances.

The fundamental purpose of insurance is to transfer risk, defined as the possibility of loss. In other words, we wish to transfer the possibility of loss to an insurer, and in exchange, we will pay that insurer a certain amount of money in the form of premiums to accept that possibility of loss. The simple wording is: we pay insurance companies money regularly in case something we love and/or need gets lost or damaged.

Let's start with the type that covers irreparable loss...

Life Insurance

Loss of life is so final that we must consider the loss irreparable. We are insuring future income against the possibility of death before the individual has a chance to earn it. If the purpose of insurance is to insure or transfer risk, then if the loss is inevitable, there is no risk and insurance is impossible. Death is inevitable, so the only possibility of insurance is to insure a life for a certain period of time. Consider:

First...what if I die before I am able to build an adequate estate to meet the needs of my family?

Second...how long will I need life insurance to cover my needs?

Third...will I be able to save enough money to meet my financial needs adequately when I retire, without the fear of running out of money before I die?

Last...how will taxes affect my accumulation of money and my potential withdrawals at retirement?

Said another way, "Will I die too soon or live too long?" There are four personal risk situations that indicate a need for life insurance:

1. Death before debt repayment when heirs do not have sufficient income to meet the obligations in the instances when they will be held responsible.

2. Spouse outliving single life pension plan recipient. If the spouse will not receive pension benefits when widowed and needs the money to support standard of living.

3. Debtor's death before having repaid money owed. Particularly true in business situations. Heirs would not be responsible for the debt, but debtor would want to repay creditor.

4. Death before reaching personal goals the client wants funded, regardless of whether s/he lives to see them fulfilled. College education is an example. Or special, expensive lessons such as ballet, figure skating, etc.

There are other situations related to the death of the primary income earner that may indicate the need for life insurance: final expenses, contingent liabilities, dependent income, education, family goals, support of parents, etc.

Closely held business risk exposures that may need life insurance are: death of a partner, death of a key employee, illiquidity of the business in the event of an owner's death. Often assets are "frozen" when one of the owner's dies. The basic types of life insurance are:

Term Insurance protects against financial loss resulting from death during a specific period of time.

Advantages:

★ Less expensive than cash value insurance in the beginning.

★ Provides more insurance protection per premium dollar initially.

★ Flexible to meet changing needs.

Disadvantages:

✗ Does not develop cash values, no savings elements to offset future costs.

✗ Cost increases as policyholder gets older.

✗ At end of term, insured may be declined for renewed coverage.

Whole Life Insurance provides insurance protection for the entire lifetime of the insured. It provides a cash value that can be used as forced savings. The premiums remain level. There can be certain tax benefits.

Advantages:

★ Provides cash values that can or may be:

    1) Used as a savings plan. (Worth considering for problem savers.)

    2) Used for financial emergencies.

    3) Borrowed against at low interest.

★ Premium level for the life of the product.

★ Tax-free income for the life of the product.

Disadvantages:

✗ More costly than term initially.

✗ Not flexible to meet changing needs.

There is a <u>Limited Pay Whole Life</u> that protects like whole life that has premium payments for a shorter period of time. During the payment period, premiums are high enough to prepay the policy.

<u>Endowment</u> insurance is a form of whole life that has very limited use since the Deficit Reduction Act of 1984–it is now limited to some qualified retirement plans. Endowment insurance is when the company

promises to pay the face amount if the insured dies within the policy period or the face amount in cash to the insured should s/he live to the end of a specified period.

Many of the detractors of whole life insurance complain about the amount of the cash value and the amount of interest paid. There is definitely merit to their arguments. The arguments crumble when the amount of cash is compared to the "nothing" most people have without it. Americans are not conscientious savers by any stretch of the imagination. If you know that is true for you, whole life deserves your consideration. Not only will you accumulate some money that you wouldn't otherwise have, you will have life insurance that will last your entire ("whole") life.

A so-called "wash" loan is when the interest paid is the same as the interest earned. For example, you pay 7% interest on the amount borrowed while you receive 7% interest on the money you have in the cash account. Hence, the notion of a "wash" which means it is 0% out-of-pocket.

Interest Sensitive whole life has dividends that are geared to current money market rates and provides many guarantees.

Adjustable whole life premiums and face amount can be adjusted every month. The policy can change from term to whole life and vice versa.

Single Premium whole life is as the name states. This insurance requires just one lump sum premium payment, usually sizeable. The tax laws were extremely favorable when this product was initially introduced. That is no longer the case. Single premium life policies are not an efficient way to purchase life insurance. Therefore, if an investor does not need the investment advantage, another type of life insurance should be purchased.

If you think single premium whole life is for you, consider the following. Most buyers of single premium whole life are age 50 or over, are in relatively high tax brackets, have a need for more life insurance, desire safe income-generating investments for retirement, and have already purchased utility stocks and municipal bonds. It is usually wise to purchase a portfolio of single premium policies so that you are not at the mercy of only one insurance company's investment decisions.

Universal Life Insurance is an "unbundled" life product with cash value that accumulates tax deferred. It includes flexible premium payments, adjustable benefits, unbundled premiums, full disclosure, and cost cutting advantages.

Advantages:

★ Flexible premium payments

★ Adjustable benefits

★ Unbundled premiums

★ Full disclosure

★ Cost effective

★ Income accumulates on a tax-deferred basis

★ Tax free income through "wash" loans

Disadvantages:

✗ Policyholder may not receive the most competitive insurance coverage or the most competitive savings vehicle.

✗ Future yield is uncertain.

✗ Compulsory form of savings reduced due to flexible premium payments.

Variable Life is a fixed-premium Whole Life policy under which the death benefit and/or cash value varies to reflect the investment experience of a separate pool of assets (separate accounts) supporting the reserves for the policies.

Premiums, less expenses and mortality (cost of insurance), are paid in a separate account where they may be invested. The separate accounts are similar to mutual funds.

There is a guaranteed minimum face amount (the original issue amount) and a maximum loan value (a percentage of the investment value) but no guarantee of minimum cash value.   Variable life is designed to provide a hedge against inflation.

Advantages:

★ Higher yield potential because of use of equities.

★ Separate accounts. The investment account belongs to the policy owner not the insurance company.

★ Full disclosure.

★ Income accumulates on a tax-deferred basis.

★ Cost effective.

★ Tax-free income through "wash" loans.

Disadvantages:

✗ The policy owner has no control over investment fluctuations but assumes the investment risk.

✗ The policy owner has no control over the investment selections.

Variable Universal Life Insurance combine all features of Universal Life and Variable Life. The policy owner selects the type of investment. The policy owner may be allowed to switch from one investment to another during the year.

Advantages:

★ Flexible premium

★ Investment choice

★ Higher yield potential

★ Separate accounts

★ Full disclosure

★ Income accumulates on a tax-deferred basis

★ Cost effective

★ Tax-free income through "wash" loans

Disadvantages:

✗ The policy owner assumes the investment risk.

Considerations When Buying Tax-Advantaged Insurance

1. Policies should be purchased for long-term needs such as for accumulating a college fund (good for individuals who have trouble saving), a retirement fund, or for building an estate. These goals cannot be met unless the policy is allowed to accumulate tax-deferred savings over a number of years. In other words, leave the cash value alone unless being used for the intended purpose!

2. Investing in a variable policy should only be made by investors willing to monitor their investment closely and invest aggressively enough to out-perform the money market yields. Gains on investment switches in a variable policy are not currently taxable.

3. Most policies include a substantial charge for withdrawals in the early years. Municipal bond mutual funds, which impose no withdrawal penalty, are generally a more attractive tax-advantaged investment for those who want liquidity and do not need insurance.

And there you have it...this represents the array of life insurance products to choose from. Now, for the big question: How much life insurance do you need? Frankly, there's no definitive way to know with absolute certainty, but here's one approach:

Simplified Approach to Determine Life Insurance Needed

Cash Needs:

1) Funeral expenses, estate taxes, and other expenses incurred after death. $_____(1)

2) Total non-mortgage debt. $_____(2)

3) Emergency fund (with one income, this becomes more important than with two incomes). $_____(3)

4) College fund. $_____(4)

5) Subtotal: Add line 1-4 $_____(5)

6) Available assets: such as savings and life insurance. $_____(6)

7) Total cash needs: subtract line 6 from 5 $_____(7)

Income Needs:

8) Annual after-tax income of wage earners prior to either spouse's death. $_____(8)

9) Annual after-tax income needed after one spouse's death: line 8 x 75%* $_____(9)

10) Survivor's Social Security benefits, in any. $_____(10)

11) Other income, including after-tax wage of surviving spouse. $_____(11)

12) Total annual income shortage: subtract lines 10 and 11 from line 9. $_____(12)

13) Amount of insurance needed to provide income shortage on line 12. Divide income shortage (line 12) by a projected interest rate (4% may be a realistic percentage). [Line 12 + .04] $_____(13)

14) Total cash needs from line 7. $_____(14)

15) Total life insurance needed. Add Lines 13 & 14. $_____(15)

*This percentage is simply an average estimate. The percentage could increase or decrease depending on the amount of mortgage payments, educational expenses, etc.

Health Care Insurance

Health care insurance coverage is an essential element of the personal financial planning process because of the umbrella of protection it provides for your financial plan.

Assume you have done everything possible to set up a fully operational personal financial plan: You have an effective spending plan; you keep track of all expenditures; you have several ongoing investment and retirement plans; and so forth. Imagine what would happen to all of this if you or a member of your family became seriously ill. There is no doubt that without adequate health care insurance, all of your accomplishments and goals could be wiped out! Health care insurance coverage is a product no effective financial plan should be without. While such insurance is intended to help you through the economic strains of serious illness or injury, it is more important to think of it as a vehicle for protecting your existing assets and financial plans.

Disability Insurance

Another absolutely *essential* part of any financial plan. This is the often forgotten element. Significant financial contributors to the family income need to be protected in the event of illness or injury. The policy should pay 60% to 70% of an insured's income. For reduced premiums, elect a long waiting period (90 days or more) if and only if you have adequate money to pay the bills during the waiting period. What good is money in 90 days if you'll go belly-up in 30 days?

A word about the calculation of the waiting period. If you elect a 30-day waiting period, this is the time period for which you will never receive any money. Disability insurance is paid monthly. So, after waiting 30 days your—deductible time period—you must wait another 30 days to earn money towards a payment from the insurance company. Then allow a 1-2 weeks for paperwork processing and post office delivery time. This means, if everything goes swimmingly, with a 30 day waiting period, you'll get your first check about ten weeks after you get sick or injured.

If your employer does not pay you during this time period, you're in "deep yogurt." Borrowing from friends and relatives is not a really viable solution because when you get paid from the insurance company, it will be for 30 days only. And you will undoubtedly need that money for current expenses. So choose your waiting period based on your situation and circumstances, not because of the cost of the premium (at least not entirely because of the premium).

Auto Insurance

A policy is needed that provides a minimum of $100,000 for a single injury, $300,000 for all injuries, and $100,000 for property damage. The rule of thumb is to drop collision coverage when the premium is equal to 10% or more of the auto's value. You need to decide based on your ability to get a down payment for a new vehicle in the event of a total loss. Avoid duplicate medical coverage. Insured may qualify for one or more discounts the insurance company offers such as for air bags, passive restraints, defensive driving school attendance, etc. Ask your insurance agent.

Homeowner's Insurance

Insure a minimum of 80% of the home's replacement cost (excluding land), and at least $300,000 against liability suits. Caution: If a taxpayer runs a business out of the home, an insurance rider to the current homeowner's policy or a separate insurance policy should be considered.

Umbrella Liability Policy

Personal liability coverage is included in both auto and homeowner insurance and may be adequate for most people. However, if an insured has substantial assets, consideration should be given to purchasing an umbrella liability policy. A $1 million policy may cost less than $250 per year.

Insurance Advice

Do the following:

★ Take the maximum deduction you can afford. Increasing the deductible on a car's collision insurance from $100 to $500, for example, could reduce the premium cost by 25%.

★ Ask the agent or company about qualifications for discounts.

★ Term life insurance should be considered. Initial premiums of such policies are usually 10% to 90% cheaper than whole life contracts.

★ Try to get health insurance through a group policy or from an employer, professional association, or union. Group coverage is often cheaper than individual policies. Also, this will prevent your individual premium from going up if you have to use the coverage often. If over age 50, check with the American Association of Retired Persons (202) 872-4700.

Don't do the following:

✗ Don't confuse the guaranteed rate with the projected rate used to forecast the future cash value of a life insurance policy. Most insurers guarantee a return of only 4% to 5%.

✗ Don't switch among cash-value life insurance policies on impulse or solely because an agent is urging you to do so. Fees and agent commissions will often outweigh a slightly higher return. When cash value life insurance policies are switched, it is usually only the new agent who truly benefits. Be very careful in this regard. The unscrupulous abound.

✗ Don't buy life insurance principally as an investment. The primary goal should be the best insurance coverage. Exceptions: Single premium whole life and variable life insurance may be attractive as tax-deferred investments. In general, it's still best to get insurance for insurance and make your investments elsewhere. (Don't put all your eggs in one basket, remember?)

The quintessential approach to insurance protection is to cover those potential losses that you don't have the money to handle on your own. And no more than that.   Proper insurance protection needs your IMMEDIATE attention because your entire financial plan depends on the proper protection being in place when its needed.   Insurance is an unusual "commodity" in that you can only buy it while you don't need it.   That sets insurance apart from everything else we purchase.

So, let's not get caught without safeguards, let's get our coverage in place...now.   The success of your entire financial plan depends on it.

Plan For Retirement

Retirement planning is a key element of financial planning. To be effective, it should begin relatively early and involve a strategy of systematically accumulating retirement funds.

The first step in retirement planning is to set your retirement goals. Fact: In order to lend direction to your retirement plan, you should begin by defining your goals; the things you want to do in retirement, the standard of living you want to maintain, and the level of income you would like. And *when* you want to retire. If you don't know when you will begin to draw on your retirement monies, you cannot get an idea of how much you need to save and invest.

The final step is to formulate an investment program that will enable you to build up your required retirement nest egg. This usually involves creating some systematic planning (putting away a certain amount each year) and identifying the types of investment vehicles that will best meet your retirement needs.

Employer-sponsored and self-directed are the two basic types of retirement programs. There are several types of "qualified plans" within these two options. A qualified plan is a plan that has met certain qualifications set by Congress which allow them to have tax advantages. That can include part or all of the contribution being tax-deductible in the year the contribution is made, and earnings being tax-deferred until paid out to the plan participant. Some of the qualified plans are:

Employer-Sponsored Programs

Profit-Sharing Plans—An arrangement in which the employees of a company participate in the company's earnings. Contributions from profit-sharing plans can be invested in annuity contracts, stocks, bonds, or in securities issued by the employing company.

401(k) (salary reduction) **Plans**—An agreement under which a portion of a covered employee's pay is withheld and invested in an annuity or other qualified form of investment; the taxes on both the contributions and the account earnings are deferred until the funds are withdrawn.

Thrift and Savings Plans—A plan established by an employer to supplement pension and other insurance fringe benefits, which the company makes contributions in an amount equal to a set proportion of the employee's contribution.

Pension Plans—A retirement account set up by an employer for its employees. If funded, the benefits are paid out of funds from insurance or annuities specifically set aside in advance. If unfunded, the benefits are paid out of the current income of the business.

Simplified Employee Pension Plans (SEPs)—The employer may make contributions to an employee's IRA account. Annuities are commonly used to fund SEPs.

Section 457 Deferred Compensation Plans
1) Employees of states, counties, and municipalities may set up an arrangement where the employer agrees with each employee to reduce his/her pay by a specified amount and to invest the deferrals in one or more investments (possibly insurance as one).
2) These amounts will be distributed to the employee upon death, retirement, or termination of employment.
3) The investments in a Section 457 plan are owned by the employer.
4) The employee then relies on the public entity to provide those funds at the specified time, not the insurance company or other investment outlet.
5) Deferred Annuities are a popular investment for these types of plans.

403(b) Tax-Sheltered Annuities (TSAs)
1) Employees of nonprofit organizations 503(c)(3) and public schools may have an arrangement where the employer agrees with each employee to reduce his/her pay by a specified amount and to invest in an Annuity contract for the employee.
2) These accounts are owned by the employee and are nonforfeitable and will be paid upon death, retirement, or termination of employment.
3) All monies invested and accumulations of interest are tax-deferred until receipt. This is also called a Tax-Deferred Annuity (TDA).

Government Regulations abound with regard to qualified plans. The Employee Retirement Income Security Act (ERISA), also known as the Pension Reform Act, was passed in 1974 with the intention of insuring workers who are eligible for pensions would actually receive such benefits. The law also permits uncovered workers to establish individual tax-sheltered retirement plans. Some of the key elements of ERISA are:

a) Eligibility must be determined and the nondiscrimination requirements regarding age and sex must be taken into consideration.

b) Normal retirement age is essential in estimating costs.

c) Benefit formula is commonly 50% to 70% of the employees' average compensation in the five to ten years immediately preceding retirement.

d) Maximum benefits are required in plans for which the benefits for key employees may be greater than for other employees.

e) Supplemental benefits are those such as death, withdrawal, disability or other benefits during the pre-retirement period.

f) Employee contributions must be determined to be contributory or non-contributory.

>Contributory=the employee bears a portion of the cost of the plan.

>Non-contributory=the employer pays the total cost of the plan.

g) Vesting allows the employee to be able to withdraw his/her contributions plus interest if he/she discontinues employment. The employer's contributions may be from 0% to 100% vested depending on the length of service and the plan schedule.

h) Method of distribution is specified in the plan.

A **Defined Benefit Plan** is a qualified pension plan that guarantees a specified benefit level at retirement.

A **Defined Contribution Plan** is a plan of any type which is based solely on the contributions to that plan. The benefits are not determined until retirement.

Self-Directed Retirement Programs

Individual Retirement Accounts (IRAs) is a plan in which an individual contributes money from his/her income and defers any taxes on the interest that accumulates. Whether an individual's contributions are deductible or not depends on whether he/she is already participating in an employer-maintained retirement plan and the level of income.

Changes to the IRAs came in two forms with 1997 tax legislation, there were changes made to the traditional IRA and a new IRA was created.

The traditional IRA has increased limits on tax-deductible contributions. Beginning for the 1998 calendar year, the phase-out for tax-deductible contributions will increase (over seven years) to $80,000-$100,000 for couples and $50,000-$70,000 for individuals. This is up from $40,000-$50,000 and $25,000-$35,000 respectively. The pre-59½ distributions will not incur the 10% premature distribution penalty if the withdrawal is for educational expenses or the purchase of a first home (withdrawal limited to $10,000 for this purpose).

Further, couples in which both spouses work but only one has an employer-sponsored retirement plan will be treated more fairly. The spouse without a plan will not be penalized by the spouse with the plan and will be allowed to contribute a fully deductible $2,000 to an IRA. To take advantage of this, joint income must be below $150,000.

The new IRA–Roth IRA–will allow taxpayers who otherwise do not qualify for traditional IRAs to put $2,000 per year into this new IRA. Contributions to the Roth IRA are not deductible, but accumulations and withdrawals are income tax free if contributions remain in the account for a minimum of five years. (Like having a 0% capital gains rate for these assets.) The 10% premature distribution penalty applies until age 59½. As with the traditional IRA, the 10% penalty does not apply to pre-59½ distributions if the withdrawal is for educational expenses or the purchase of a first home.

Roth IRA contributors can pull out an amount up to their original contribution at any time (even before 59½) without penalty and there is no requirement to begin taking distributions at 70½ as currently required for traditional IRAs. Phase-out for couples is between $150,000 and $160,000 of adjusted gross income and between $95,000 and $100,000 for individuals.

IRAs may be funded by Certificates of Deposit (CDs), mutual funds, annuities, or common stocks. Not life insurance.

Self-Directed Retirement Programs (cont'd)

Simplified Employee Pensions (SEPs) Can be self-directed or employer-sponsored. A self-employed individual can make contributions to a SEP even if he/she has no employees. The maximum contribution is 15% of earned income. However, the actual percentage is 13.0435% because the tax code requires the contribution percentages to be calculated after all contributions are deducted from income.

For example, $50,000 of income times 13.0435% equals a maximum contribution of $6,522. The tax code's computation method must first subtract the contribution from income ($50,000 minus $6,522=$43,478) and then multiply $43,478 times 15% which equals a maximum contribution of $6,522.

Employees wages do not have to be reduced by the contribution amount.

Self-Employed Plans (HR 10 or Keogh Plans) A plan in which a self-employed individual may contribute part of his/her earned income into a retirement plan and deduct those contributions from present taxable income. The earnings accrue on a tax-deferred basis. The maximum contribution is 25% of earned income. However, the actual percentage is 20% because the tax code requires the contribution percentage to be calculated after all contributions are deducted from income.

For example, $50,000 of income times 20% equals a maximum contribution of $10,000. The tax code's computation method must first subtract the contribution from income ($50,000 minus $10,000=$40,000) then multiply $40,000 times 25% which equals a maximum contribution of $10,000.

There is an alternative to the qualified plans: **Private Pension Plans**

A private Pension Plan can give you a retirement income just like a qualified plan. But the Private Pension Plan, under current tax law, does not have the restrictions and limitations imposed by Congress and the IRS.

For example:	Qualified Plan	Private Pension Plan
Limit on your contributions	Yes	None
Penalty for distribution before age 59½	10%	None
Must distribute money in plan (and pay taxes) when you reach 70½ (except Roth IRA)	Yes	No
Tax-free death benefit	No	Yes
Tax-free retirement income	No	Yes

What is a Private Pension Plan?

The Private Pension Plan is a life insurance plan especially designed to produce a maximum retirement income both pre- and post-retirement death benefits utilizing the several tax advantages that are available only through life insurance. Why should you consider a Private Pension Plan?

No Government Red Tape:

Since 1974, Congress has changed the law almost every year further restricting qualified plans–often limiting benefits for business owners. For example:

- Maximum 401(k) or SEP contributions by an owner have been reduced by 75%. (IRC sec. 401(a)(30))
- Qualified plans must provide equal benefits for everyone.
- All eligible employees must be included.
- Shorter vesting schedules for participants.
- Top heavy plans penalized.

Qualified Plan Expenses For An Employer Continues To Go Up:

- Annual changes in the law have required expensive plan amendments.
- Mandatory vesting and participation requirements requires employer contribution for employees who may leave within a few years.
- Plan administration costs increase each year.

While all of this is going on, the government is reducing your retirement income options:

- Tax-free income from Municipal Bonds are subject to the alternative minimum tax.
- Virtually every other retirement income option is subject to income tax.

Advantages of a Private Pension Plan

★ Increased tax rates will not affect your benefits:

Benefits are paid by using withdrawals to basis and then taking policy loans. Under current law, such withdrawals and policy loans are not subject to income tax. **Tax-free** income is *not* affected by taxes no matter how high rates go!

★ Flexible payment schedule:

Provided you pay enough to keep the policy in force, you can vary payments each year. Adding additional amounts in future years will increase the amount available at retirement.

★ Tax-deferred growth:

Life insurance allows the cash value to grow tax deferred. That is, no tax is paid on the gain while the values are accumulating. And if policy loans are used at retirement, no tax is paid then either! At death, the policy loan is repaid tax free with the remaining death benefit paid to your family.

A Private Pension Plan may be of benefit to business owners. This plan has no reporting requirement. Therefore, you can maximize your qualified plan and contribute to a Private Pension Plan without being penalized. There is no reporting of income if you use the loan method at retirement. The Roth IRA income will be reported as non-taxable. The Private Pension Plan is "private",—no one knows how much is being put in or withdrawn.

Consult your Financial Advisor to see if the Private Pension Plan will benefit you.

Social Security and Retirement Planning

Social Security is an important source of income for retired people; however, if it is the only source, the retiree is likely to find that his or her standard of living will be considerably less than what had been hoped for.

No one can accurately predict the amount of social security benefits that will be paid twenty to thirty years from now. (It is possible that the social security system will be out of funds.) For retirement planning purposes, however, it seems reasonable to expect social security to provide the average retired wage earner, who is married, with about 40 to 60 percent of the wages that he or she earned in the year before retirement commenced.

Of course, this assumes that the retiree has had a full career working in covered employment. Therefore, social security should be viewed as a foundation for your retirement income. By itself, social security is insufficient to allow a retiree to maintain a pre-retirement standard of living. For people who earn in excess of the wage, a lower percentage of total pre-retirement wages will be replaced by social security.

Consequently, both average and upper-middle income families must plan to supplement their social security retirement benefits with income from other sources. The popular sources were discussed earlier in this chapter.

While everything discussed in this chapter is worth absorbing, the *most* important things about your retirement plan is how and when you save your money. Yes, we're back to saving money again. Experts almost all had one overriding piece of advice on how to save more. Expressed in various ways, it boils down to this: Put aside a set amount regularly.

The sooner, the better.

If putting aside a set amount regularly is the best savings rule, the second best one is: Do so early.

That's because of the way compound interest works. The longer it can compound, the bigger the return. Consider the example of Jane and Joe, who are the same age:

Jane starts saving $600 a year when she is 21. She does so until she is 28. In other words, she puts away $4,800 (8 years times $600). From then until she is 65 she doesn't save another dime. But she leaves the money where it can earn 10 percent interest compounded annually and doesn't touch it until she is 65.

Joe saves nothing from age 21 to 28. But when he is 29 he decides to emulate Jane. He puts $600 away each year for 37 years; that is, until he is 65. He has put away a total of $22,200 (37 years times $600), also putting it where it can earn 10 percent interest compounded annually.

At 65 who has more money?

The amazing answer is: Jane.

Jane's bottom line at age 65, because of compounded interest, will be $256,650. Joe's will be $217,830—or $38,820 less than Jane's. A dollar short, by comparison.

So, be sure to actually plan your retirement but it is best to execute your plan as early as possible!

Tenth Principle of Financial Control:

Plan Your Estate
(or take the government's plan)

E state planning is the process of planning for the disposal of property during life, at death, and after death in a manner that best carries out a person's desires, while minimizing income, gift, and death taxes. Did you get all that? That was quite a mouthful that I'll attempt to explain fully in this chapter.

Estate planning involves more than making a will or trust or placing property in joint tenancy. A good estate plan must consider taxes, probate, insurance, investments, charitable giving, and family wealth distribution. A good estate plan has two goals:

- To distribute wealth to intended heirs.
- To diminish taxes.

An estate plan should proceed on the assumption that the estate owner will die in the near future. A person with a large estate should review the plan annually. A person with a small estate should review the plan at least every five years. The reasons estate plans must be reviewed include:

- Tax laws change
- Estates grow or shrink
- People marry, divorce, remarry, die, and have children
- Minors become adults
- Beneficiaries become financially responsible or irresponsible
- *You* change
- Circumstances change

Here's an example of an estate plan that was never reviewed. In 1926, the breadwinner purchased a life insurance policy that his wife was to receive $100 a month upon his death and his daughter was to receive $100 a month. This individual died in 1990 and his wife, age 84, is "stuck" with $100 a month. Likewise, his daughter will have no alternative but to live with the terms of his estate plan. Needless to say, he had simply forgotten that these were the terms. Don't let it happen to you!

Common Techniques Used in Estate Planning:

1) Place property in joint ownership with right of survivorship.

2) Make gifts of property to family members.

3) Set up a trust in a will that provides income to the spouse for life and transfers the principal to the children upon the death of the spouse.

4) For estates over $625,000*, devise property to a Marital Deduction Trust with income to the spouse for life, the spouse having a general power of appointment over the principals. The remainder of the property to a trust with income to the spouse for life, and the balance to the children upon the spouse's death. (*The amount will incrementally increase to $1,000,000 over the next ten years–thanks to the 1997 tax legislation.)

5) Same as (4) except the spouse has a special power of appointment over the Marital Deduction Trust. This allows the grantor of the trust to control the identity of remaining beneficiaries.

6) Set up a Revocable Living Trust which can incorporate any of the above-named trusts. This gives the estate owner flexibility to control, coordinate, and distribute the estate.

7) Purchase and structure life insurance to avoid federal estate tax through the use of an irrevocable Life Insurance Trust. Surviving spouse can receive a portion and the remainder can go to the children.

8) Make charitable contributions to receive present tax benefits and to reduce the value of the estate.

Estate Planning Tips

For Older Couples:

■ Make gifts while alive to reduce the taxable estate.

■ Transfer ownership of life insurance to beneficiaries or to a trust to reduce the taxable estate.

■ Keep assets on which value has risen sharply so heirs escape income tax on past gains.

■ Set up a trust to handle finances should one or both spouses become incapacitated, or if one or both are uneasy about making financial decisions.

■ For large estates, do not leave everything to each other. This can unnecessarily expose the estate of the second spouse to die to estate tax.

For Couples With Children:

■ Write separate wills, including provisions for disbursing assets should both die simultaneously and designating who will be the children's guardian.

■ Consider setting up a trust to provide for minor children.

■ Hold some assets jointly so a surviving spouse has access to a bank account, or so an out-of-state vacation home can be passed on without the red tape of probate in that state.

For Everyone:

■ Have an accurate valuation of assets.

■ Know where all title papers are located, and understand how title to property has been taken.

■ If a person does not already have an estate plan, the laws of the person's domicile will provide one. (The government's plans I mentioned in the title of this chapter.)

- If estate planning is accomplished by a will, remember that wills are only effective at death and require a public probate process.

- Probate involves unnecessary red tape and expense. Probate can and should be avoided.

- Federal estate taxes are imposed on the right to transfer property interests at death. The taxes are paid before beneficiaries receive their inheritance.

- Many people lose sight of the fine distinction between ownership of property and controlling interest in it. For estate tax purposes, any property subject to a controlling interest will be included in the decedent's gross estate, such as an interest in a Revocable Living Trust.

- The federal estate tax rules generally apply only to estates greater than $625,000 in 1998. (Increases as follows: $650,000 in 1999; $675,000 in 2000; $700,000 in 2002; $850,000 in 2004; $950,000 in 2005; and $1,000,000 in 2006.)

- Spouses in all states can give or leave an unlimited amount of property to each other tax free.

- It is not always good to rely on the marital deduction. It may increase the estate tax payable on the death of the second spouse.

- The easiest and least expensive way to reduce gross estate is with a lifetime giving program. Gifts up to $10,000 can be made without incurring any gift tax liability. Spouses can "split" gifts, raising the amount to $20,000.

- Do not rely on joint ownership entirely. Property may pass to unintended heirs, planning opportunities are limited, and there are stepped-up basis considerations.

- Most states have their own death and gift taxes. Always consider state laws when planning.

- Gifting property to a minor can be difficult. In order to make a gift to a minor, an account must be established under the Uniform Gifts to Minors Act or Uniform Transfers to Minors Act.

- A private annuity can give cash flow and move property out of the estate. In a private annuity, property is sold to someone who ordinarily would have inherited it, such as a child. The buyer takes legal title and promises to make payments. Part of each payment received will be a tax-free return of investment.

- Unmarried individuals need an estate plan. Most discussions of estate planning focus on traditional married couples and ignore the special problems of single, divorced, and widowed individuals.

- Small business owners get a special tax break in paying their estate taxes when a closely held business or farm makes up 35% of the value of the gross estate.

Estate planning is one of the most neglected areas of financial planning and it doesn't have to be because plans are not complicated or expensive to create. It is entirely possible to do most or all of it yourself. There's plenty of help available—from books to computer software. Choose a method and get it done before your heirs get stuck with the government's plan.

Eleventh Principle of Financial Control:

Pay Fewer Taxes!
(Take all deductions you're entitled to.)

"Anyone may so arrange his affairs that his taxes shall be as low as possible; he is not bound to choose the pattern which will best pay the Treasury; there is not even a patriotic duty to increase one's taxes."

Appeals Court Judge
Learned Hand, 1934

Tax planning never stops. And it makes sense for everyone—not just the wealthy.

No one can take a job, buy a house, get married, raise children, invest money or start a business without plunging into a sea of tax implications. While those implications are daunting, there are helpful principles you can use to keep your head well above water.

Principles to Keep in Mind

- Don't think of tax planning as something you do only once a year when preparing to file your tax return. To be really effective, tax planning must continue throughout the year.

- Professional advisers caution you to be wary of making financial decisions—especially investment decisions—for tax reasons alone. It's the total payoff that counts, not the immediate tax savings. Tax-free earnings from a municipal bond, or "muni," for example, may yield less over time than the after-tax gain from a taxable investment.

■ Develop a long-term financial and tax strategy, and make short-term moves to fit that strategy.

■ In shopping for investments, remember the difference between **tax-deferred**, and **tax-free** (tax exempt) income. If the income is tax-free, such as the interest from a municipal bond, you'll never have to pay federal tax on it. If the income is tax-deferred, such as retirement plan earnings or the increase in a stock's value while you hold the stock, you delay paying taxes until you withdraw the plan earnings or sell the stock.

What to do on the job:

The way you handle your pay, benefits, and retirement plans has a big effect on your tax bill. The largest share of most people's taxable income is what they earn on the job. A good way to begin planning for your taxes is to look for ways to cut the taxable part of your earnings and to take advantage of benefits that give you a tax break for certain expenses, such as medical bills.

Tax-Free Benefits

Many employee benefits are like money in your pocket, yet their cash value isn't taxed. You get some tax-free benefits, such as medical insurance, automatically. Other employee benefits, such as 401(k) plans, are designed to reduce the taxable part of your income if you put your own money into them. Take time to learn what's available to you.

The law permits employers to give tax-free subsidies to employees for the cost of getting to work. It's up to the employer to do this. The limit is $60 a month for bus or train fare or for the cost of sharing a van that seats at least seven people. An employer may subsidize up to $155 a month of an employee's cost of parking at the job—tax free.

Taxable Benefits

Many employee benefits are taxable, including the personal use of company car, a personal trip on the company plane, a country club membership and group term life insurance that exceeds $50,000.

Generally, your employer may choose not to withhold taxes on your non-cash income, so you may have to pay more tax on April 15th than you expected. Keep track of the value of the income, and be prepared to come up with the tax money. You may even have to pay estimated taxes on these benefits, if they increase your earnings substantially.

Deferred Compensation & Flexible Spending Plans

Flexible spending and deferred compensation plans offer an advantage that you may not notice. They reduce adjusted gross income, or AGI, which is the basic for many limits on personal exemptions and itemized deductions.

If you earn a high income and are subject to broad limits on personal exemptions and itemized deductions, you may minimize or escape the effects of the limits by lowering your AGI. You may also slip past the specific limits on certain deductions, such as medical expenses and IRA contributions.

Flexible spending plans give you the *option* of taking part of your pay as *tax-free fringe benefits*. The choices may include health insurance, payment of medical costs that aren't covered by insurance, life insurance, and dependent care. The arrangement, sometimes called **cafeteria** or **salary-reduction plans,** are valuable because they let you cut your taxable income without losing the use of the money.

If you contribute to one of these plans, it is taken out of your paycheck and put into an account for you. You aren't taxed on the money you set aside. As you run up bills for those benefits, the company either pays them or reimburses you out of your account.

Here's how it works: Suppose you set aside $1,000 for medical bills that aren't paid in full by insurance. You aren't taxed on the $1,000. If your federal tax rate is 28 percent, you've saved $280 to pay medical bills (more, if you take state and local income taxes into account). That's cash you probably couldn't save by taking the $1,000 as an itemized deduction, because of the severe limit on medical deductions.

A flexible spending plan is a great way to cut taxes, but going into one takes some study. You must decide before a year starts how much to set aside during that year. You'll need to review previous expenses to come up with a good estimate. Once your decision takes effect, you can't alter it unless there's a change in your family status. There's a major drawback to a flexible spending plan: If you don't spend all the money in your account by year's end, you lose all of the unused amount. It isn't refunded to you or carried over to the next year.

Deferred Compensation

Many companies offer special plans to executives who can afford to wait for some of their money until they retire or leave the company. To take advantage of these plans, you may elect in a written agreement to defer part of your salary or your bonus before you earn it.

You aren't taxed on this income, or on any interest it may accumulate, until you receive it years later, presumably when your tax rate will be lower. However, under certain circumstances, the money taken out at a later date may be subject to Social Security taxes. Before making such an agreement, you may want to consult an adviser. One caveat: since the deferred compensation is not protected by pension fund regulations, you may want to make sure the company will have the money to pay you when the time comes.

Investment Tax Planning

Don't overlook the tax consequences when figuring the return on your investments. Financial advisers recommend that you make investment choices based on factors such as return on investment, level of risk, and portfolio diversity, not on tax avoidance. Still, investing your money to gain the best possible return after taxes is a vital part of any investment decision.

Capital Gains

A *capital gain* is the profit that results from buying and selling stock or property. Capital assets include everything you own for investment and personal use—stocks and tax-exempt bonds, your home and furnishings, jewelry, cars, and collectibles.

Gains from selling these assets are usually taxable. Losses are not deductible unless you show you held the item for investment and not for personal use. You also need complete records for all of these transactions and expenses.

In one of the most significant changes in the tax law, the 1997 Tax Legislation, alters the capital gains tax rates. For assets sold on or after July 29, 1997 and held for a minimum of 18 months, the capital gains tax rate drops from 28% to 20%. For couples with adjusted gross income of less than $41,200, the new capital gains tax rate will be 10%—down from 15%.

The new lower capital gain rate of 20% will also apply to assets sold on or after May 7th but before July 29, 1997 and held for a minimum of twelve months. Assets sold on or after July 29, 1997 and held 12-18 months will pay capital gains at the 28% rate. Assets sold on or after July and held less than twelve months will pay ordinary income tax rates (no capital gains treatment).

The top rate will drop to 18% for assets purchased in or after 2001 and held for five years. This means the earliest possible year in which long-term capital gains can be sold with the highest capital gain rate at 18% will be in the year 2006.

The top capital gains tax rate for collectibles remains at 28%.

Assets Sold	Holding Period	Capital Gains Rates
On or after May 7th, before July 29, 1997	12 months	20%
On or after July 29, 1997	12-18 mos.	28%
On or after July 29, 1997	18 months	20%
On or after July 29, 1997	12 months	39.6%
In the year 2006	5 years	18%

Consult your financial adviser for strategies on how you can reap the most savings from lower capital gains rates.

Giving Can Be A Gain

If you donate appreciated property, such as stock or a house, that you've held for over a year, you may deduct the market value and avoid capital gains tax on the appreciation. If a stock's value has dropped, you can sell it, take the capital loss and donate the proceeds of the sale.

Once your child is over age 14, you can save taxes by giving the child stock that has appreciated in value while you owned it. The child sells the shares and pays capital gains tax at a lower rate than yours.

Tax Shelters and Passive Income

Passive income or losses are derived from businesses in which you aren't an active participant. These include limited partnerships, rental real estate and other rental activities that you don't help manage. Most tax shelters are passive partnership ventures designed to let investors deduct or take tax credits for more dollars than they actually put up in cash. Shelters are designed for high-income taxpayers willing to take risks.

The 1986 tax act eliminated most of these tax shelters. Losses from passive investments may now be deducted only from income from similar ventures. The losses can no longer shelter other income. That is, they can't be deducted from active income, such as wages and salaries, or portfolio income, such as interest, dividends, and capital gains. Losses not taken can only be deducted when the passive investment is sold or disposed of in a taxable transaction. A gift is not a taxable transaction.

Tax Planning for Tax-Free Investments

Federal, state, and local governments pay interest that is partly or fully tax free. For some taxpayers, these are some of the best investments around.

"Munis" is a catch-all term for bonds sold by state and local governments. The interest they pay is generally exempt from federal tax and is usually exempt from state and local taxes if the bonds are issued in your home state. If you sell munis for a profit, however, you'll have to pay a capital gains tax.

Municipal bonds, like any investment, are not risk free. Tax free bonds that pay the highest interest are issued by governments and agencies with low credit ratings. Financial advisers suggest sticking to highly rated bonds unless you're ready to take risks.

Some mutual funds invest only in tax-exempt bonds. Form 1099-Div will tell you whether your income is tax exempt or not. If you're receiving Social Security benefits, tax-exempt income is added back to your other income to determine whether your Social Security income is taxable.

Treasury Offerings

Investments in U.S. treasury securities are considered to be the safest available. The interest is subject to federal income tax, but not to state and local taxes.

Treasury bills have terms of up to a year. **Treasury notes** have terms from two to ten years, and **Treasury bonds** have terms of more than ten years. Interest on notes and bonds are taxed annually, but interest on bills are taxed at maturity, or when bills are sold.

Figuring Your Yield

Before buying tax-free bonds you need to know whether the yield, or interest rate of income, is better than the after-tax yield on a corporate bond or on another taxable investment. Take federal, state, and local tax rates into account, especially in high tax states such as California and New York.

Tax-free bonds may not offer much advantage if you're in the 28 percent federal tax bracket. But the higher your marginal tax rate is, the more likely you are to receive a greater net yield on a tax free investment than on one that's taxed.

A taxpayer in the 31 percent bracket, for example, needs a taxable return of about 8.69 percent just to match a tax-free yield of 6 percent. But if you're in the 36 percent bracket, you'll need to find a taxable return of 9.37 percent just to equal that 6 percent tax-free yield. These numbers don't reflect state and local taxes or what happens when you receive Social Security benefits. The taxable return must be even higher if you take those factors into account.

Tax Implications of Other Federal Investments

U.S. savings bond interest is subject to federal tax, but not to state and local taxes. You can elect to pay tax annually or defer until maturity.

Federal zero-coupon bonds pay you no interest until maturity. But you pay annual federal tax on the interest as though you received it each year.

Ginnie Mae securities issued by the Government National Mortgage Association, are shares in the income from a pool of mortgages. The interest is subject to federal, state, and local income taxes.

Tax Planning for Homeowners

The home you own isn't just a roof over your head, it's a tax shelter too. Tax deductions for home loans and real estate taxes are among the best tax breaks available. You can deduct interest payments on as much as $1 million of the money you borrow to buy, build, or improve your main residence and one other home.

Home Equity Loans

You can also deduct the interest on home equity loans of up to $100,000. This kind of loan is like a second mortgage, secured by the value of your home. The amount is based on the market value of the home, less what you owe on your first mortgage. The big tax break is that you may use the loan money for just about anything and still deduct the interest. You can buy a car, finance a college education, or pay off credit cards.

If you use a loan secured by your home to provide money for investments or for your business, the interest may be deductible as investment interest or business interest. The deduction won't be limited by the $100,000 ceiling. The risk of home equity loans is putting up your home as security. You can lose your home if you can't keep up the loan payments.

Refinancing Your Mortgage

If you refinance your mortgage, your new deduction is limited to the interest on the principal you've paid off. Let's say you refinance a $100,000 mortgage after ten years. You've reduced the principal to $90,000 but you borrow $100,000 and pay off the first loan. Generally, you may deduct interest paid on $90,000 as a home equity loan. The alternative minimum tax also limits interest deductions if you borrow more than you owed on your old mortgage and you didn't spend the proceeds on home improvement.

Remember, if you refinance to pay a lower interest rate, you also will reduce your interest deductions. That can increase your tax, although the overall effect should be money saved.

Selling Your Home

The tax law is tough on home sellers. If you make a profit selling your primary home, it is taxable as a capital gain. If you sell at a loss, the loss isn't deductible. Most home sellers can avoid ever having to pay the profit, however, by spending all the proceeds on buying and improving another home. The proceeds or **adjusted sales price**, are what you get after you subtract selling costs. Generally, you "roll over" the gain on the sale of your home and defer the tax no matter how many times you move, as long as the next home costs at least as much as the price you got for the one before. This tax deferral applies to the sale of only your main home, not to other residences such as a vacation cabin. The restrictions are:

- You must buy and move into the new home within two years before or two years after selling the previous home.
- You can roll over the gain only once every two years unless you move because your job location changes.

If you die and leave your home to an heir, the deferred taxes owed on past home sales are wiped off the slate and are never paid.

If you don't buy another home after you sell, or if you don't put all your profit into the next one, you owe tax. That's why it's very important to have good records of all the money you spend to buy, sell, and improve homes. Those expenses reduce your potential profit. Unfortunately, maintenance such as painting and repairs such as patching the roof don't count as improvements.

Keep home sale records as long as you own the home or a replacement. Figuring the profit from selling a home is tricky, especially if you roll it over more than once.

Under the current tax legislation, a taxpayer age 55 or older will be able to exclude from federal income tax up to $250,000 of the gain from the sale of a principal residence; married couples filing jointly can exclude up to $500,000. The exclusion will be allowed each time someone who meets the eligibility requirements sells a primary residence, but not more than once every two years.

Family Tax Planning

Children & Taxes

Major tax breaks are available to parents who can save taxes by giving money to their children and even by hiring them. A key to family tax planning is the children's age.

Transferring Money to Children

You may be able to reduce overall family taxes by shifting some of your taxable income to children aged 14 and older. This reduces taxes because children are taxed at their own rate which is typically lower than the parents rate.

A child under age 14 with unearned (investment) income over $1,300 is taxed at the parents rate. So you benefit from shifting income to a child under age 14 only if the income is under the limit. Giving a child tax-exempt bonds doesn't shift taxable income. But the child may pay a lower capital gains tax than you when the bonds are sold.

State laws, called Uniform Gifts to Minors Act and the Uniform Transfers to Minors Act, let parents and others give money to a child under a custodian's control. Banks and financial service companies have information about the way these accounts work.

You and your spouse can each give up to $10,000 each a year (in addition to normal support) to a child, or anyone else, without federal gift taxes. Remember that legally the money becomes the child's. You can't decide how it's spent after the child reaches legal age.

Parents Who Employ Their Children—The Benefits

- A child can earn up to $4,150 tax free in 1997; $6,150 tax free if $2,000 is contributed to an IRA.
- Wages earned by the child are taxed at the child's rate (the next $24,650 of wages are taxed at 15%).

- Children under age 18 who work for their parent's unincorporated business are not subject to Social Security tax withholding (savings of 15.3% of wages) or FUTA.
- Children's wages are deducted as a business expense by the parent-employer if:

1) Work is done in connection with the parent's trade or business (or income-producing property).
2) Child actually renders services to trade or business.
3) Payments to the child are reasonable in relation to the services rendered, and
4) Payments are actually made.

Tax Savings—Real Estate

Own A Home (See Appendix for home buying tips.)

There are four factors that make owning a home a good investment and America's leading tax shelter:

1) Long term inflation, economic growth, and population growth push real estate values upward.
2) Most of the purchase price can be financed and the interest is tax deductible, effectively cutting the interest cost by the taxpayer's marginal tax rate.
3) Any taxes on the profit are deferred until actual sale of the home and can be deferred further by buying another home.
4) On the sale of a home at age 55 or over, the first $250,000 in profit is completely tax free.

Buy House Or Apartment For College-Age Child

- By treating this house/apartment as a second home, parents can deduct mortgage interest and property taxes. Also, the child will have a free place to live.
- By setting the house up as a rental property, parents can write off up to $25,000 of losses on the property if their AGI is $100,000 or less.

When the child finishes school, the investment will likely have appreciated in value.

- Hire the child as the property's resident rental manager. Parents can pay the child a reasonable salary and deduct it as a business expense. Remember, up to $4,150 of the child's salary will be tax free or taxed at the child's rate.

- *Important: Parents must charge and collect rents from the child and other renters.*

Sell Home to Children

A retired parent can sell the home to the children on the installment basis and rent it back from them. Remember, if the parent is at least age 55, up to $250,000 of the gain is tax free.

The parent can get extra cash from the down payment and installment payments. The children can get a tax deduction even with a positive cash flow by creating a rental loss through depreciation and other expenses.

If the parent is in a lower tax bracket than the children because of retirement, the interest received will be deductible at the higher rate of the children. This cuts the overall family tax bill.

Be prepared: The IRS scrutinizes family deals closely, so the house must be sold for a reasonable market price and rented back for a reasonable market rent.

Five Tax-Wise Ways to Help A Child Buy a Home

- *Give the child the down payment.* Make sure the gift of the down payment is less than the annual limitations so there is no gift tax. If the child is married, parents can give $20,000 to their child and another $20,000 to the child's spouse for a total of $40,000 each year.

- *Lend the child money to "buy down" the mortgage interest rate.* By making an advance deposit with the mortgage lender, the child may qualify for a lower mortgage rate. This can make the difference between getting the loan or not. The low starting interest rate will gradually rise, but hopefully so will the child's income.

- *Buy the home and rent it to the child with an option to buy.* This entitles the parent to deduct cash expenses and depreciation. The parent should charge close to a fair market rent.

- *The child buys the home, but borrows the down payment from the parent.* On a loan of less than $10,000, the parent need not charge any interest. On a loan of less than $100,000, interest must be charged only if the child's net investment income exceeds $1,000.

- *Enter into an equity sharing arrangement with the child.* Parent and child each put up part of the down payment and take title as co-owners. Each pays a proportionate share of the mortgage installments and upkeep. The child must also pay fair rent to the parent for the parent's share of the house. The parent can deduct his share of the rental expenses. If the home goes up in value, the profit is shared.

Own A Business

Some financial experts say, "if you are not self-employed, do whatever you have to do to get that way." Some advantages: lower tax rate, fringe benefits, retirement, and income shifting. All the laws in this country in some way protect and aid the entrepreneur. Especially the tax laws. Ours is a capitalist-free enterprise system. It is not a coincidence or capricious that the tax laws favor businesses.

Have you ever asked yourself why it is that people in business get tax breaks?

In 1913, Income Tax was established under the Sixteenth Amendment to the Constitution and the Internal Revenue Tax Code (tax laws) came into existence. The Congress then and practically every Congress since then have written the tax codes in favor of business. The two major reasons the codes are written in favor of businesses are:

1) When a person in business pursues a profit and there is economic activity (the spending of money on telephone, gasoline, supplies, insurance, entertainment, etc.), they help stimulate the economy.

2) Business have large lobbying and special interest groups that make sure the government doesn't forget the importance business plays in furthering the economy. Since the small business person truly is the backbone of our economy, you should consider your efforts to pursue profit as helping to strengthen the free enterprise system that is the very foundation of this country.

If you decide to start a business, you should consult your financial and tax advisers on how to make your business profitable and beneficial.

Dealing With The IRS

The organization of the IRS is important. A taxpayer must understand whom they are dealing with, what power that entity has, and how to protest an action by that agency. The IRS has four major functions:

- The IRS assists taxpayers in filing accurate returns and processing tax returns that are filed.
- The IRS determines taxes due by auditing tax returns to make sure all taxpayers are complying with existing law.
- The IRS collects taxes from an estimated twenty million delinquent accounts and identifies the estimated ten million tax-payers who have failed to file tax returns.
- The IRS conducts investigations, prosecutes cases, and handles taxpayer appeals.

You may deal with one or more of the following:

Taxpayer Service Representatives can answer your questions on how to prepare your tax return, which form to use, or where to call for further assistance.   These individuals cannot work out collection agreements, hear your appeals, or answer questions about your audit.

Revenue Agents are normally encountered during the audit. In auditing your tax return, the revenue agent is bound by IRS policy and cannot take into account the hazards of litigation. The job of the revenue agent is to verify the information you have reported on your tax return. Therefore, they cannot consider whether your witness will provide credible testimony in court.

Special Agents investigate criminal tax matters. They have the power to execute and serve search and arrest warrants, issue subpoenas and summonses, or seize property subject to forfeiture. Run to your nearest tax attorney if a special agent is involved in your case.

Tax Law Specialists are the lawyers or CPAs who work in the National Office of the IRS in Washington, D.C. They are the experts in the law of specialized area or industry. These individuals issue private letter rulings, answer technical advice requests or write IRS regulations.

Revenue Officers are charged with collecting delinquent taxes. They can seize your property without a court order, issue federal tax liens, and levy your wages.

Appeals Officers have the power to review the audit report and negotiate a settlement with you. They can consider hazards of litigation, and therefore have more latitude in negotiating a settlement than a revenue agent.

District Counsel Attorneys are charged with the job of litigating cases on behalf of the IRS when a taxpayer files a petition with the U.S. Tax Court. They have the broadest discretion in negotiating a settlement. It is important to remember whom you are dealing with because the individual may or may not have the authority to grant the relief you are seeking.

IRS Audit Defense & Protection Record Statute of Limitation

The best defense for an audit is adequate records. Your tax records need to be retained for as long as your tax return is subject to an audit. The statute of limitations runs three years from the filing date of your tax return. The statute of limitations runs for six years if the IRS discovers that you understated income by more than 25 percent. There is not statute of limitations on fraud.

Barring any flagrant irregularities, tax records may be discarded after six years. However, according to some of the nation's top financial planners and investment advisers, copies of your tax returns should be kept forever. In the event of your death, your heirs may need evidence that taxes have been paid on certain items—stock dividends, bond interest, real estate income—so they won't be hit with back taxes.

Records are food for substantiation in an IRS audit. But for your protection, you should have representation. There are attorneys, accountants, CPA's and enrolled agents that can properly represent you in an audit or tax court. You should never represent yourself. The laws are complicated. To represent yourself in an audit is like doing your own root canal. The best audit defense and protection are to have adequate records and professional representation.

Taxpayer Bill of Rights

The law provides taxpayers with more protection and safeguards when dealing with the IRS. Here's a rundown of the provisions designed to prevent potential IRS abuses. You have the right to:

1) Receive an explanation of the examination and collection processes and your rights under these processes before or at the initial interview for the determination or collection of tax.

2) Have representation at any time during these processes by a person who may practice before the IRS, except in certain criminal investigations.

3) Make an audio recording or receive a copy of such a recording of an interview for the determination or collection of tax.

4) Reasonably rely on written advice from the IRS that was provided in response to your specific written request.

5) File an application for relief with the IRS Ombudsman in a situation where you are suffering or about to suffer a significant hardship as a result of the manner in which the IRS is administering the tax laws.

6) Receive a written notice of levy, no less than 30 days prior to enforcement, which explains in non-technical terms, the levy procedures and the administrative appeals and alternatives to levy which are available to you.

Changes in the law define the costs that may be awarded in court proceedings when you prevail in court and have exhausted all administrative remedies available within the IRS. Also, you may bring suit against the IRS for civil damages for certain unauthorized collection actions.

I do not suggest that the information contained in this section is easy to digest or easy to implement. I do strongly suggest that an understanding of the material is imperative if you want to be in control of your own destiny and not be forced to rely on the advice and recommendations of "professionals" and acquaintances. Professionals is in quotation marks because knowledge is the only way to make certain you are, in fact, dealing with professionals. Think about it, if you don't know, how do you determine that someone else does? Remember, the ramifications of your tax planning or lack thereof are too far-reaching to leave to chance. Know for yourself!

Afterword

In conclusion, I'd like to talk about the notion of being "rich." Recent literature has revealed that the vast majority of those who become rich do so working at "ordinary" jobs like you and I have. The difference between those that achieve wealth and those who don't is the way they *think* about money. And what they *do* with their money. And, of course, the *actions* they take.

For the most part, people who have become millionaires didn't get there by acting rich. One elderly woman, who's worth about $5 million, still worries about writing $1,000 checks, said Grossman with the Edward Jones brokerage firm in Houston.

To look at his affluent clients, you'd never know they're wealthy, Grossman said. The elderly woman drives a car that's about 10 years old. Even those who aren't so motivated to be rich—and a life dedicated to hoarding isn't good—can learn valuable lessons from how these people accumulated wealth.

These aren't the people profiled in *Lifestyles of the Rich and Famous* who are seen lugging shopping bags along the world's toniest shopping avenues. Their addresses aren't likely to be found on a list of the richest neighborhoods.

But an increasing number of people are adopting the lifestyles of these inconspicuous millionaires: Living below their means, limiting debt and sticking to a savings plan with monotonous regularity. Many consumers have gotten the message that there's no substitute for good old-fashioned money management principles. Baby boomers, who have dedicated a large chunk of their life to spending, and are now realizing they can't depend on Social Security and any other institutional safety nets to sustain them in retirement. Baby boomers are finally getting the message.

Two baby boomers, Donald Moore and Marcia Engle, got the message early in life and have built a comfortable life just by managing their money conservatively. They live in a two-story, four-bedroom home. Managing money with discipline hasn't deprived them of enjoying life. They take a couple of vacations a year, which typically cost about $3,000. They pay with cash.

"Our sure-fire formula isn't complicated," said Moore, 50, a sales representative, who became a veterinary technician after she was laid off in 1991 during downsizing. The key points of their plan are:

- They live on 75 percent of their income and save the rest using mutual funds, most of which is invested in stocks.
- They minimize their credit card bills and paid off their mortgage early. They drive older vehicles—a 1983 Mazda RX-7 car and a 1986 Mazda truck.
- They max out contributions to retirement savings plans and seek professional investment advice.

"We had some goals in mind where we didn't want to work the rest of our lives and we just were savers, rather than spenders," Engle said. "We just felt that putting away 25 percent of our after-tax income may get us to where we want to go." A growing number of people are following the financial principles used by this married couple. More people have decided they must abandon the hope of winning the lottery or turning up in the will of a wealthy relative. If they want to accumulate wealth, they'll have to do it themselves.

We've got to learn to live within our means. It does no good to covet Bill Gates's lifestyle. We need to become comfortable with who we are, what we are and what we are making. If we aren't comfortable with that, we need to educate ourselves and change. Otherwise, we're not going to have a happy life.

While we don't have control over whether we're Microsoft chief Bill Gates, there are some things we can do to make the most of our limited income, such as starting to save early to take advantage of the compounding effect of money.

Experts said young people are starting to care more about saving for several reasons:

- Their own retirement is staring them in the face and they realize the cost of a long retirement is huge.
- This is the first century that people have really retired. Before this century, most people worked until they died.
- They don't have faith that Social Security and other government aid will be around for them.
- They realize that they have been living from paycheck-to-paycheck and are now atoning for their spending excess.

The effort by workers to save feverishly for their retirement has helped boost the stock market to unprecedented heights and fueled the sale of mutual funds. Over one-third of our total assets in the mutual fund industry are in formal retirement plans like IRAs and 401(k)s. This provides additional security for those of us who invest in the stock market because huge fluctuations are less likely. A repeat of 1987 is highly unlikely because of the sheer volume of money currently invested in the stock market.

That notwithstanding, ideas surrounding proper money management are akin to those concerning good nutrition: They're well-accepted but most people have trouble sticking with the program. Like one speaker said: "It's not that we don't know, we don't show." We all know what to do, we just don't do it all the time.

One client of mine makes $70,000 a year and he's always broke. He says, "It looks like I should have enough money, but it's always gone."

Despite their concern and savings efforts, people still aren't putting away enough, financial advisers say. "The baby boomers are saving about 38.5 percent of what we think they should save in order to maintain the same standard of living they're living now." said Gardener of Merrill Lynch. "They're still consuming."

The national savings rate—savings as a percentage of disposable personal income—averaged 4.3 percent in 1996, down from an average 4.7 percent in 1995, said Bill Gilmer, economist at a branch of the Federal Reserve Bank of Dallas. For 1997, the savings rate was 3.7 percent in the first quarter and 4.2 percent in the second quarter.

One reason some baby boomers aren't saving enough is because some are among the *sandwich generation*: squeezed by having to provide for elderly parents and finance their children's college education at the same time.

The man who makes $70,000 a year has learned a harsh lesson: No matter how much money you make, it still won't be enough if you don't manage it properly. "We have no other savings and seem to just get by each month" the man said. "I have a company pickup, I don't have to pay any maintenance or insurance. I feel like I should be ahead of the game."

He's recently found there's a payoff to keeping a close eye on expenses. "A little bit of savings on a regular basis can add up and I don't even miss it," he said. This man finally accepted his reality and knows that there will never be a *good* time to prepare for his future. We all have ongoing financial challenges in our lives (being *sandwiched* for instance). The real challenge for us is the face that looks back in the mirror every morning—ourselves. We must get control of ourselves if our financial situation will ever get under control. Probably sounds simplistic or like common sense. Unfortunately, often times, 'common sense' is very uncommon.

One more common-sense lesson should be added: The pursuit of money really isn't everything. It takes time to make money and time can only be used for one thing at a time. It's imperative that we all choose well.

Values of those who accumulate wealth are different from those who are broke. Most wealth-builders know that material items aren't the most important thing. Having a good family life and being happy with their day-to-day life and having a home they're comfortable with are the most important things. Larger doesn't mean better to them.

There was a time when I was impressed by brand new luxury automobiles (always driven by others). I'm no longer impressed because, I now know that too often individuals driving these types of vehicles are drowning in debt, have little or no savings, and are usually poorly protected. Many of them are only three paychecks away from financial disaster. Though I can afford a luxury car today, I wouldn't dream of doing that with my money. My money has more important work to do. What about yours?

I wish you good financial health.

Appendixes

Monthly Expenses

Date Due	Item	Week	*Month	Year
	Savings, investments			
	Housing (rent or mortgage)			
	Utilities–electricity			
	Utilities–gas or other fuel			
	Utilities–water and sewage			
	Utilities–telephone			
	Utilities–garbage			
	Insurance–property			
	Insurance–home			
	Insurance–medical			
	Insurance–disability			
	Insurance–automobile			
	Insurance–other			
	Medical–doctor			
	Medical–dentist			
	Medical–drugs			
	Medical–other			
	Home Furnishings			
	Household maintenance			
	Child care			
	Household help			

Date Due	Item	Week	*Month	Year
	Transportation–gasoline			
	Transportation–maintenance			
	Transportation–bus, taxi			
	Food and groceries			
	Meals eaten out			
	Alcohol and tobacco			
	Clothing			
	Laundry/dry cleaning			
	Hair care			
	Spa or health club			
	Recreation or entertainment			
	Cable TV			
	Business Expenses			
	Contributions			
	Education or self improvement			
	Dept. store payments			
	Credit card payments			
	Monthly loan payments			
	Oil company payments			
	Other monthly installments			
	Miscellaneous			
	Total			

*Multiply amount per week X 4.3

Periodic Expenses

Item	Month(s) needed	Amount Spent last year	Amount budgeted this year	Average monthly amount
Automobile License, Inspection, and Maintenance				
Insurance Automobile, Life, Homeowners, Other				
Gifts Christmas, Birthdays, Other				
Medical Checkups Physical, Dental, Diagnostic Tests				
Organizational Dues Clubs, Professional Associations				
Subscriptions Magazines, record & book clubs				
Taxes Income, Real Estate				
Vacations				
Totals				

Determine Income

	Per Week	Biweekly	Per Month	Per Year
Paycheck #1				
Paycheck #2				
Paycheck #3				
Paycheck #4				
Tips				
Commission				
Interest				
Dividends				
Gifts				
Annuities				
Social Security				
Retirement Benefits				
Child Support				
Alimony				
Public Assistance				
Veterans' Benefits				
Other				
Totals				

(See reverse side for hints and more information.)

Record **all** your income (no cheating!).

Then figure out the monthly amount. Always calculate your spending on a monthly basis for ease of analysis. For persons who are paid on a weekly or biweekly basis, monthly income can be figured as 4 1/3 times the weekly rates. Having said that, it is better to estimate low and use the four week income as your baseline. This leaves the extra four weekly or two biweekly paychecks as a "bonus" that can be set aside for savings, used to meet emergency expenses, or for a special occasion such as Christmas expenses. (One client of mine has been treating these checks as "bonuses" for years and it has done wonders for his savings. Since he uses these checks for his vacations and all-occasion gift-related expenses, his savings remain untouched for these expected expenditures.)

When your earnings are irregular, base your estimate on your previous income and current prospects. If your income fluctuates sharply–as it may for seasonal workers, commissioned salespersons, farmers, and other self-employed people–play it safe by making two estimates. Work out the smallest and largest numbers you can reasonably expect. Plan firm on the basis of the low-income figure, then consider how you will use additional amounts if they are available.

Money Web Sites

Various Money Topics	http://www.homearts.com
Vanguard Mutual Funds	http://www.vanguard.com
The Dollar Stretcher	http://www.stretcher.com
Your Time & Money	http://www.sacbee.com
Save on Airline Tickets	http://www.senior-center.com
Discount Air Fares & More	http://www.travelocity.com
Common Consumer Law	http://wwwconsumerlaw.com
Consumer World	http://www.consumerworld.org
Thinking Rich	http://www.chron.com
Cash Management	http://www.cccsmoneymatters.org
Understanding Mutual Funds	http://www.ivyleaguefinsvs.com
Basics of Financial Planning	http://www.chitrib.webpoint.com
Quicken Investment Primer	http://www.quicken.com
Understanding Investing	http://www.cdnglobal.com
2.5 Million Book Titles	http://www.amazon.com

Car Shopping	http://www.autoweb.com
Get "inside" 55 car models	http://www.carpoint.msn.com
Low Cost Stock Trades	http://www.etrade.com
Microsoft Investor	http://www.investor.msn.com
Discount Groceries	http://www.netgrocer.com
Auction House	http://www.onsale.com
Up-to-minute Stock Info	http://www.quote.com
Interactive Calculators	http://www.financenter.com
Calculate Interest Rates	http://www.interest.com
Mortgage Lenders & More	http://www.hsh.com
Investing Glossary	http://www.investorwords.com
Low Cost Air Fares	http://www.priceline.com

Mortgages: A How-To Guide

Whether you're buying a home or refinancing, lenders don't make it easy to find a good deal. Here's help.

Perhaps the most consequential step you will take when buying a home or refinancing the one you have is finding a mortgage and a lender you can afford to live with. Your monthly mortgage payment, after all, will almost surely be your heaviest financial burden. The job of shopping for a mortgage is a financial rite of passage one with many potential perils. Lenders offer low initial teaser rates on adjustable mortgages that can climb steeply. Some are beginning to add onerous penalty clauses to loan contracts that can cost you money if you refinance. And there is no shortage of "experts" eager to sell you advice that can be both expensive and self-serving. Indeed, any missteps you make on the way to signing a mortgage contract can have costly repercussions. Even within a single region, interest rates on a 30-year mortgage can vary by as much as two percentage points, according to HSH Associates, a Butler, N.J., firm that tracks the rates. Choose a mortgage that charges a half-percentage point too much, or select one that has a maturity that is too long or too short and you could end up paying tens of thousands of dollars more than necessary over the life of the loan. For example, a 30-year loan at 7 percent interest on a principal of $100,000 will cost you $239,500 by the time you make your final payment, but a loan for the same amount at 8.5 percent will end up costing $37,000 more.

What kind of mortgage?

Competition among lenders has given consumers a broad array of choices, but it hasn't made comparison-shopping easy. Mortgages now come in nearly every conceivable combination of interest rate, duration, and fee structure.

Which loan makes the most sense depends on how long you plan to remain in the home and the monthly payment you can afford. If you live in a city where co-operative apartments are common, you will probably have fewer options. Lenders consider not just the credit-worthiness of the co-op buyer, but the underlying financial health of the corporation that issues the building's shares.

The conventional 30-year fixed-rate mortgage has been the perennial favorite of borrowers, and it's more popular than ever as both buyers and refinancers scramble to lock in today's low rates. It offers homeowners the peace of mind of knowing that even if economic conditions cause interest rates to rise sharply, their payments will remain steady.

But in these footloose days, relatively few people remain rooted in a home for a lifetime. If you plan to relocate within a few years, you may find an adjustable-rate mortgage (ARM) less costly. The most common ARMs recalibrate interest once a year, based on an index of benchmark Government bond rates.

ARMs made sense for many borrowers in the early 1980s, when interest rates were high and volatile. Their lower initial rates were often the only way that many people could afford to buy a home. But lately the spread between conventional and ARM has narrowed to two points or less, too small to be worth the risk of paying more next year *unless it's the only way* your income qualifies you for a mortgage.

One breed of ARMs is worth considering. These maintain a fixed interest rate for a specified number of years typically 3, 5, 7, or 10 and then adjust annually for the balance of the loan. Multi-year ARMs may be well suited for consumers planning to relocate within or soon after the mortgage's initial period. In fact, the average mortgage is paid off in just seven years because the borrower moves to a different home or refinances the loan in that time.

Multi-year ARMs permit borrowers to lock in, at least for a few years, a lower initial interest rate than they could get for a fixed-rate mortgage. And, because the monthly payment on an ARM is lower, banks are able to qualify borrowers with a smaller income.

How to lower your costs

While the interest rate you get will be the biggest factor determining the ultimate cost of your mortgage, lenders have other ways of upping your costs. You can save thousands of dollars and much frustration by getting pre-qualified and pre-approved for a mortgage and by minimizing transaction fees. Here's where to look for your best opportunities to save:

Pre-qualification. Lenders expect borrowers to spend no more than 28 percent of their pretax income on total housing costs, including mortgage payments, insurance, and taxes. Housing costs plus all other long-term debt, such as car payments and student loans, should not exceed 36 percent (41 percent if FHA) of your gross income.

Ask your broker or a potential lender whether you would qualify for a loan before you begin shopping. It can save you time by focusing your attention on properties that realistically fit your budget.

Preapproval.

As you get closer to selecting the property you want, consider lining up a bank that will give you its provisional agreement to grant you a loan. Preapproval can boost your bargaining power with the seller, who knows that with financing in place you can close the deal quickly.

There are some pitfalls to beware of. While many lenders pre-approve free, some charge a fee. At some banks, pre-approved borrowers pay $50 or more for a credit check but they won't get their money back if they decide to go with another lender.

Locking in the rate. Before you pay to lock in a given interest rate for a specified time period, ask if the lender will be willing to lower it if interest rates decline. And get a commitment for at least 60 days. A

30-day lock-in won't be of much use if you're just beginning to shop for a home. (It can typically take 45 days to complete all the paperwork.)

Points and other closing costs. Your lender may be willing to offer you a lower interest rate on a mortgage that includes points (each point equals a one percent fee paid at the closing on the total amount of the loan).

Your lender is required to give you a good-faith estimate of the charges you'll be expected to pay to finalize the loan for property appraisal, title insurance, credit reports, and the like. Carefully review every item on the list. Sometimes lenders will pad the bill with unnecessary charges, such as courier fees. Other items, like title insurance, you may be able to buy more cheaply on your own.

The mortgage-insurance ripoff. Borrowers who put down less than 20 percent of the purchase price must have mortgage insurance to protect the lender in the event of default. But avoid "lender paid" insurance, a way some lenders get you to make extra premium payments. It sounds good because the premium is part of your tax-deductible monthly mortgage interest payment. But you go on paying even after your equity exceeds 20 percent of the home's value. You should pay the premiums separately in cash and drop the policy once your home equity crosses that 20 percent threshold.

Prepayment penalties. Watch out for mortgages that impose a penalty if you decide to pay them off ahead of schedule. With more consumers trading in their old mortgages for lower-cost new ones, lenders want to write the penalties into more loan contracts something many states currently allow them to do.

Accelerated payment. Another thing you shouldn't have to pay extra for: biweekly payments that help you pay off your loan faster. Some lenders will charge you a fee of $500 or so to arrange it. If you make the extra payments yourself, however, you can avoid the fee and the obligation that comes with the lender's program. Borrowers who regularly make 13 monthly payments a year instead of 12 can pay off a 30-year mortgage in about 22 years and save some $52,000 over the life of a $100,000 loan.

Finding good advice

Lenders' advertisements in the local newspaper can give you a flavor of what's available, but don't buy on the strength of an ad alone. The most attractive advertised rates are often a tease to draw customers in; and, in any event, the rates in effect when the ad is published will likely be different when you are ready to deal.

One good source of up-to-date information is HSH Associates' "Homebuyer's Mortgage Kit," which you can receive by mail. For $20, you get a clearly written booklet on how to shop for a mortgage and detailed information on loan rates from 80 percent of the lenders in the market you select. (Call 800 873-2837 or check www.hsh.com.)

Where else can you turn? A good real-estate agent should know which banks offer the best terms in the community where you are buying. And the National Association of Mortgage Brokers can help you locate a mortgage broker in your state who specializes in sifting through the competing offers of several banks. (Write to the Association at 1735 N. Lynn St., Suite 950, Arlington, Va. 22209.)

Be careful before you act on any expert's advice. A real-estate agent may refer you to a lender that is affiliated with his or her company. And mortgage brokers don't work for free: If you aren't paying their fee, the lender to whom they refer your business probably is. A good real-estate professional can help save you time, money, and anxiety, but you have too much at stake to trust an expert to do your homework for you. (Principle #1, Educate Yourself)

Glossary

Alpha A measure of selection risk (also known as residual risk) of a mutual fund in relation to the market. A positive alpha is the extra return awarded to the investor for taking a risk, instead of accepting the market return. For example, an alpha of 0.4 means the fund outperformed the market-based return estimate by 0.4 %. -0.6 means a fund's monthly return was 0.6 % less than would have been predicted from the change in the market alone.

Alpha Equation The alpha of a fund is determined as follows:
[(sum of y) - ((b)(sum of x))] / n
where: n =number of observations (36 mos)
b = beta of the fund
x = rate of return for the S&P 500
y = rate of return for the fund

American Depositary Receipts Certificates issued by a U.S. Depositary Bank, representing foreign shares held by the bank, usually by a branch or correspondent in the country of issue. One ADR may represent a portion of a foreign share, one share or a bundle of shares of a foreign corporation. If the ADR's are "sponsored," the corporation provides financial information and other assistance to the bank and may subsidize the administration of the ADR's. "Unsponsored" ADR's do not receive such assistance. ADR's carry the same currency, political and economic risks as the underlying foreign share; the prices of the two, adjusted for the SDR/ordinary ratio, are kept essentially identical by arbitrage. American Depositary Shares (ADS) are a similar form of certification.

American-style Option An option contract that can be exercised at any time between the date of purchase and the expiration date. Most exchange-traded options are American style.

Amortization The process of fully paying off indebtedness by installments of principal and earned interest over a definite time.

Analyst Employee of a brokerage or fund management house who studies companies and makes buy and sell recommendations on their stocks. Most specialize in a specific industry.

Annual Percentage Rate (APR) The cost of credit on a yearly basis expressed as a percentage.

Annual Report Yearly record of a publicly held company's financial condition. It includes a description of the firm's operations, its balance sheet and income statement. SEC rules require that it be distributed to all shareholders. A more detailed version is called a 10-K.

Appraisal Fee The charge for estimating the value of property offered as security.

Appraisal A professional opinion, usually written, of the market value of a property, such as a home, business, or other asset whose market price is not easily determined. Usually required when a property is sold, taxed, insured, or financed.

Appraiser A person qualified by education, training, and experience to provide appraisals. also called evaluator.

Appreciation The increase in value of an asset. opposite of depreciation. see also capital appreciation, return.

Arbitrage Profiting from differences in the price of a single security that is traded on more than one market.

Arms Index Also known as TRading INdex (TRIN):= #advancing issues/#declining issues Total up volume/total down volume. An advance/decline market indicator. Less than 1.0 indicates bullish demand, while above 1.0 is bearish. The index often is smoothed with a simple moving average.

Assignment The receipt of an exercise notice by an options writer that requires him to sell (in the case of a call) or purchase (in the case of a put) the underlying security at the specified strike price.

At the Money An option is at-the-money if the strike price of the option is equal to the market price of the underlying security. For example, if XYZ stock is trading at 54, then the XYZ 54 option is at-the-money.

Autoregressive Using previous data to predict future data.

Average An arithmetic mean of selected stocks intended to represent the behavior of the market or some component of it. One good example is the widely quoted Dow Jones Industrial Average, which adds the current prices of the 30 DJIA's stocks, and divides the results by a predetermined number, the divisor.

Average Maturity The average time to maturity of securities held by a mutual fund. Changes in interest rates have greater impact on funds with longer average life.

Back Office Brokerage house clerical operations that support, but do not include, the trading of stocks and other securities. Includes all written confirmation and settlement of trades, record keeping and regulatory compliance.

Balloon Payment A large extra payment that may be charged at the end of a loan or lease.

Banker's Acceptance A short-term credit investment created by a non-financial firm and guaranteed by a bank as to payment. Acceptances are traded at discounts from face value in the secondary market. These instruments have been a popular investment for money market funds.

Basis The price an investor pays for a security plus any out-of-pocket expenses. It is used to determine capital gains or losses for tax purposes when the stock is sold.

Basis Points Refers to yield on bonds. Each percentage point of yield in bonds equals 100 basis points. If a bond yield changes from 7.25 % to 7.39 %, that's a rise of 14 basis points.

Bear An investor who believes a stock or the overall market will decline. A bear market is a prolonged period of falling stock prices, usually by 20% or more.

Bear Raid A situation in which large traders sell positions with the intention of driving prices down.

Beta (Stocks) Measure of a stock's risk in relation to the market. 0.7 means a stock price is likely to move up or down 70 % of the market change; 1.3 means the stock is likely to move up or down 30 % more than the market.

Beta Equation (Stocks) The beta of a stock is determined as follows:
[(n) (sum of (xy))]-[(sum of x) (sum of y)]
[(n) (sum of (xx))]-[(sum of x) (sum of x)]

where: n = # of observations (24-60 months)
x = rate of return for the S&P 500 Index
y = rate of return for the stock

Beta (Mutual Funds) The measure of a fund's risk in relation to the market. 0.7 means the fund's total return is likely to move up or down 70 % of the market change; 1.3 means total return is likely to move up or down 30 % more than the market.

Beta Equation (Mutual Funds) The beta of a fund is determined as follows:
[(n) (sum of (xy))]-[(sum of x) (sum of y)]
[(n) (sum of (xx))]-[(sum of x) (sum of x)]

where: n = # of observations (36 months)
x = rate of return for the S&P 500 Index
y = rate of return for the fund

Blow-off Top A steep and rapid increase in price followed by a steep and rapid drop in price. This is an indicator seen in charts and used in technical analysis of stock price and market trends.

Breakout A rise in a security's price above a resistance level (commonly its previous high price) or drop below a level of support (commonly the former lowest price.) A breakout is taken to signify a continuing move in the same direction. Can be used by technical analysts as a buy or sell indication.

Bull An investor who thinks the market will rise.

Bull Market A market which is on a consistent upward trend.

Buy Down A lump sum payment made to the creditor by the borrower or by a third party to reduce the amount of some or all of the consumer's periodic payments to repay the indebtedness.

Buyout Purchase of a controlling interest (or percent of shares) of a company's stock. A leveraged buyout is done with borrowed money.

Call Option An option contract that gives the holder of the option the right (but not the obligation) to purchase, and obligates the writer to sell, a specified number of shares of the underlying stock at the given strike price, on or before the expiration date of the contract.

Capital Expenditures Amount used during a particular period to acquire or improve long term assets such as property, plant, or equipment.

Capital Gain When a stock is sold for a profit, it's the difference between the net sales price of securities and their net cost, or original basis. If a stock is sold below cost, the difference is a capital loss.

Capital Loss The difference between the net cost of a security and the net sale price, if that security is sold at a loss.

Cash Dividend A dividend paid in cash to a company's shareholders. The amount is normally based on profitability and is taxable as income. A cash distribution may include capital gains and return of capital in addition to the dividend.

Cash and Equivalents The value of assets that can be converted into cash immediately, as reported by a company. Usually includes bank accounts and marketable securities, such as government bonds and Bankers' Acceptances. Cash equivalents on balance sheets include securities (e.g., notes) that mature within ninety days.

Cash Flow In investments, it represents earnings before depreciation amortization and non-cash charges. Sometimes called cash earnings. Cash Flow from operations (called Funds From Operations (FFO) by real estate and other investment trusts, is important because it indicates the ability to pay dividends.

Changes in Financial Position Sources of funds internally provided from operations which alter a company's cash flow position: depreciation, deferred taxes, other sources, and capital expenditures.

Churning Excessive trading of a client's account in order to increase the broker's commissions.

Closed-End Credit Generally, any loan or credit sale agreement in which the amounts advanced, plus any finance charges, are expected to be repaid in full over a definite time. Most real estate and automobile loans are closed- end agreements.

Closing Purchase A transaction in which the purchaser's intention is to reduce or eliminate a short position in a stock, or in a given series of options.

Closing Sale A transaction in which the seller's intention is to reduce or eliminate his long position in a stock, or a given series of options.

Collateral Also referred to as security. Property that is offered to secure a loan or other credit and that becomes subject to seizure on default.

Commission The fee paid to a broker to execute a trade, based on number of shares, bonds, options and/or their dollar value. In 1975, deregulation led to the creation of discount brokers, who charge lower commissions than full service brokers. Full service brokers offer advice and usually have a full staff of analysts who follow specific industries. Discount brokers simply execute a client's order--and usually do not offer an opinion on a stock.

Common Stock/other Equity Value of outstanding common shares at par, plus accumulated retained earnings. Also called shareholders' equity.

Community Reinvestment Act (CRA) This act encourages banks to help meet the credit needs of their communities for housing and other purposes, particularly in neighbor-hoods with low or moderate incomes. The banks are also expected to maintain safe and sound operations.

Confidence Indicator A measure of investors' faith in the economy and the securities market. A low or deteriorating level of confidence is considered by many technical analysts as a bearish sign.

Confidence Level The degree of assurance that a specified failure rate is not exceeded.

Confirmation The written statement that follows any "trade" in the securities markets. Confirmation is issued immediately after a trade is executed. It spells out settlement date, terms, commission, etc.

Convergence The movement of the price of a futures contract toward the price of the underlying cash commodity. At the start, the contract price is higher because of the time value. But as the contract nears expiration, the futures price and the cash price converge.

Corner a Market To purchase enough of the available supply of a commodity or stock in order to manipulate its price.

Cosigner Another person who signs for a loan and assumes equal liability for it.

Coupon Rate In bonds, notes or other fixed income securities, the stated percentage rate of interest, usually paid twice a year.

Covered Call A short call option position in which the writer owns the number of shares of the underlying stock represented by the option contracts. Covered calls generally limit the risk the writer takes because the stock does not have to be bought at the market price, if the holder of that option decides to exercise it.

Covered Put A put option position in which the option writer also is short the corresponding stock or has deposited, in a cash account, cash or cash equivalents equal to the exercise of the option. This limits the option writer's risk because money or stock is already set aside. In the event that the holder of the put option decides to exercise the option, the writer's risk is more limited than it would be on an uncovered or naked put option.

Credit The promise to pay in the future in order to buy or borrow in the present. The right to defer payment of debt.

Creditworthiness A creditor's measure of a consumer's or company's past and future ability and willingness to repay debts.

Credit Card Any card, plate, or coupon book that may be used repeatedly to borrow money or buy goods and services on credit.

Credit History A record of how a person or company has borrowed and repaid debts.

Credit Scoring System A statistical system used to determine whether or not to grant credit by assigning numerical scores to various characteristics
related to creditworthiness.

Current Assets Value of cash, accounts receivable, inventories, marketable securities and other assets that could be converted to cash in less than 1 year.

Current Liabilities Amount owed for salaries, interest, accounts payable and other debts due within 1 year.

Current Ratio Indicator of short-term debt paying ability. Determined by dividing current assets by current liabilities. The higher the ratio, the more liquid the company.

Current Yield For bonds or notes, the coupon rate divided by the market price of the bond.

Day Order An order to buy or sell stock that automatically expires if it can't be executed on the day it is entered.

Debt/equity Ratio Indicator of financial leverage. Compares assets provided by creditors to assets provided by shareholders. Determined by dividing long term debt by common stockholders' equity.

Decile Rank Performance over time, rated on a scale of 1-10. 1 indicates that a mutual fund's return was in the top 10 % of funds being compared, while 3 means the return was in the top 30 %. Objective Rank compares all funds in the same investment strategy category. All Rank compares all funds.

Declaration Date The date on which a firm's directors meet and announce the date and amount of the next dividend.

Deferred Taxes A non-cash expense that provides a source of free cash flow. Amount allocated during the period to cover tax liabilities that have not yet been paid.

Default Failure to meet the terms of a credit agreement.

Depreciation A non-cash expense that provides a source of free cash flow. Amount allocated during the period to amortize the cost of acquiring long term assets over the useful life of the assets.

Derivative Security A financial security, such as an option, or future, whose value is derived in part from the value and characteristics of another security, the underlying security.

Detrend To remove the general drift, tendency or bent of a set of statistical data as related to time.

Difference from S&P A mutual fund's return minus the change in the Standard & Poor's 500 Index for the same time period. A notation of -5.00 means the fund return was 5 percentage points less than the gain in the S&P, while 0.00 means that the fund and the S&P had the same return.

Discount An amount deducted from the regular price for those who purchase with cash instead of credit. Don't confuse this with the discount on a bond which is different

Distributions Payments from fund or corporate cash flow. May include dividends from earnings, capital gains from sale of portfolio holdings and return of capital. Fund distributions can be made by check or by investing in additional shares. Funds are required to distribute capital gains (if any) to shareholders at least once per year. Some Corporations offer Dividend Reinvestment Plans (DRP).

Dividend Reinvestment Plans (DRP) Plans offered by many corporations for the reinvestment of dividends, sometimes at a discount from market price, on the dividend payment date. Many DRP's also allow the investment of additional cash from the shareholder. The DRP is usually administered by the company without charges to the holder.

Divergence When two or more averages or indices fail to show confirming trends.

Dividend Distribution of a portion of a company's earnings, cash flow or capital to shareholders, in cash or additional stock.

Dividend Yield (Stocks) Indicated Yield represents annual dividends divided by current stock price.

Dividend Yield (Funds) Indicated Yield represents return on a share of a mutual fund held over the past 12 months. Assumes fund was purchased 1 year ago. Reflects effect of sales charges (at current rates), but not redemption charges.

Dividends Per Share Dividends paid for the past 12 months divided by the number of common shares outstanding, as reported by a company. The number of shares often is determined by a weighted average of shares outstanding over the reporting term.

Dividend Reinvestment Plan Automatic reinvestment of shareholder dividends in more shares of a company's stock, often without commissions. Some plans provide for the purchase of additional shares at a discount to market price. Dividend reinvestment plans allow shareholders to accumulate stock over the long term using dollar cost averaging.

Downgrade A classic negative change in ratings for a stock, and or other rated security.

Earnings Net income for the company during the period.

Earnings Per Share (EPS) Also referred to as Primary Earnings Per Share. Net income for the past 12 months divided by the number of common shares outstanding, as reported by a company. The company often uses a weighted average of shares outstanding over reporting term.

Earnings Yield The ratio of Earnings Per Share after allowing for tax and interest payments on fixed interest debt, to the current share price. The inverse of the Price/Earnings ratio. It's the Total Twelve Months Earnings divided by number of outstanding shares, divided by the recent price, multiplied by 100. The end result is shown in percentage.

Equity The value of the common stockholders' equity in a company as listed on the balance sheet.

Equity Options Securities that give the holder the right to buy or sell a specified number of shares of stock, at a specified price for a certain (limited) time period. Typically one option equals 100 shares of stock.

European-style Option An option contract that can only be exercised on the expiration date.

Exchange The marketplace in which shares, options and futures on stocks, bonds, commodities and indices are traded. Principal US stock exchanges are: New York Stock Exchange (NYSE), American Stock Exchange (AMEX) and the National Association of Securities Dealers (NASDAQ).

Ex-Dividend Date The first day of trading when the seller, rather than the buyer, of a stock will be entitled to the most recently announced dividend payment. This date set by the NYSE (and generally followed on other US exchanges) is currently two business days before the record date. A stock that has gone ex-dividend is marked with an x in newspaper listings on that date.

Execution The process of completing an order to buy or sell securities. Once a trade is executed, it is reported by a Confirmation Report; settlement (payment and transfer of ownership) occurs in the U.S. between 1 (mutual funds) and 5 (stocks) days after an order is executed. Settlement times for exchange listed stocks are in the process of being reduced to three days in the U.S.

Exercise To implement the right of the holder of an option to buy (in the case of a call) or sell (in the case of a put) the underlying security.

Expense Ratio The percentage of the assets that were spent to run a mutual fund (as of the last annual statement). This includes expenses such as management and advisory fees, overhead costs and 12b-1 (distribution and advertising) fees. The expense ratio does not include brokerage costs for trading the portfolio, although these are reported as a percentage of assets to the SEC by the funds in a Statement of Additional Information (SAI). the SAI is available to shareholders on request. Neither the expense ratio or the SAI includes the transaction costs of spreads, normally incurred in unlisted securities and foreign stocks. These two costs can add significantly to the reported expenses of a fund. The expense ratio is often termed an Operating Expense Ratio (OER).

Expiration Cycle An expiration cycle relates to the dates on which options on a particular security expire. A given option will be placed in 1 of 3 cycles, the January cycle, the February cycle, or the March cycle. At any point in time, an option will have contracts with 4 expiration dates outstanding, 2 in near-term months and 2 in far-term months.

Expiration Date The last day (in the case of American-style) or the only day (in the case of European- style) on which an option may be exercised. For stock options, this date is the Saturday immediately following the 3d Friday of the expiration month; however, brokerage firms may set an earlier deadline for notification of an option holder's intention to exercise. If Friday is a holiday, the last trading day will be the preceding Thursday.

Finance Charge The total dollar amount paid to get credit.

Fixed Rate An approach to determining the finance charge payable on an extension of credit. A predetermined and certain rate of interest applied to the principal of a loan or credit agreement.

Fund Family The management company that runs and/or sells shares of the fund. Fund families often offer several funds with different investment objectives.

Funds from Operations (FFO) Used by real estate and other investment trusts to define the cash flow from trust operations. It is earnings with depreciation and amortization added back. A similar term increasingly used is Funds Available for Distribution (FAD), which is FFO less capital investments in trust property and the amortization of mortgages.

Futures Contract Agreement to buy or sell a set number of shares of a specific stock in a designated future month at a price agreed upon by the buyer and seller. The contracts themselves are often traded on the futures market. A futures contract differs from an option because an option is the right to buy or sell, whereas a futures contract is the promise to actually make a transaction.

Good 'Til Canceled Sometimes simply called "GTC," it means an order to buy or sell stock that is good until you cancel it. Brokerages usually set a limit of 30-60 days, at which the GTC expires if not restated.

Growth Rates Compound annual growth rate for the number of full fiscal years shown. If there is a negative or zero value for the first or last year, the growth is NM (not meaningful).

Head & Shoulders In technical analysis, a chart formation in which a stock price reaches a peak and declines, rises above its former peak and again declines and rises again but not to the second peak and then again declines. The first and third peaks are shoulders, while the second peak is the formation's head. Technical analysts generally consider a head and shoulders formation to be a very bearish indication.

Hedging A strategy designed to reduce investment risk using "call" options, "put" options, "short" selling, or futures contracts. A hedge can help lock in existing profits. Its purpose is to reduce the potential volatility of a portfolio, by reducing the risk of loss.

High Price The highest (intraday) price of a stock over the past 52 weeks, adjusted for any stock splits.

Holding Company A corporation that owns enough voting stock in another firm to control management and operations by influencing or electing its board of directors.

Indicated Dividend Total amount of dividends that would be paid on a share of stock over the next 12 months if each dividend were the same amount as the most recent dividend. Usually represent by the letter "e" in stock tables

Indicated Yield The yield, based on the most recent quarterly rate times four. To determine the yield, divide the annual dividend by the price of the stock. The resulting number is represented as a percentage.

Industry The category describing a company's primary business activity. This usually is determined by the largest portion of revenue.

Initial Public Offering (IPO) A company's first sale of stock to the public. Securities offered in an IPO are often, but not always, those of young, small companies seeking outside equity capital and a public market for their stock. Investors purchasing stock in IPOs generally must be prepared to accept very large risks for the possibility of large gains. IPO's by investment companies (closed end funds) usually contain underwriting fees which represent a load to buyers.

Insider Information Relevant information about a company that has not yet been made public. It is illegal for holders of this information to make trades based on it, however received.

In-the-money A "call" option is in-the-money if the strike price is less than the market price of the underlying security. A "put" option is in-the-money if the strike price is greater than the market price of the underlying security. For example, an XYZ "call" option with a 52 strike price is in-the-money when XYZ trades at 52 1/8 or higher. An XYZ "put" option with a 52 strike price is in-the-money when XYZ is trading at 51 7/8 or lower.

Inventory For companies: Raw materials, items available for sale or in the process of being made ready for sale. They can be individually valued by several different means, including cost or current market value, and collectively by FIFO, LIFO or other techniques. The lower value of alternatives is usually used to preclude overstating earnings and assets. For security firms: securities bought and held by a broker or dealer for resale.

Inventory Turnover The ratio of annual sales to inventory. Low turnover is an unhealthy sign, indicating excess stocks and/or poor sales.

Investment Trust A closed-end fund regulated by the Investment Company Act of 1940. These funds have a fixed number of shares which are traded on the secondary markets similarly to corporate stocks. The market price may exceed the net asset value per share, in which case it is considered at a "premium." When the market price falls below the NAV/share, it is at a "discount." Many closed end funds are of a specialized nature, with the portfolio representing a particular industry, country, etc. These funds are usually listed on US and foreign exchanges.

IRA/KEOGH Accounts Special accounts where you can save and invest, and the taxes are deferred until money is withdrawn. These plans are subject to frequent changes in law with respect to the deductibility of contributions. Withdrawals of tax deferred contributions are taxed as income, including the capital gains from such accounts.

Last Split After a stock split, the number of shares distributed for each share held and the date of the distribution.

Limit Order An order to buy a stock at or below a specified price or to sell a stock at or above a specified price. For instance, you could tell a broker "Buy me 100 shares of XYZ Corp at $8 or less" or to "sell 100 shares of XYZ at $10 or better."

Load Fund A mutual fund with shares sold at a price including a sales charge--typically 4 % to 8% of the net amount indicated. Some "no-load" funds have distribution fees permitted by article 12b1 of the Investment Company Act; these are typically 0.25%. A "true no-load" fund has neither a sales charge not 12b1 fee. A load implies that the fund purchaser receives some investment advice or other service worthy of the charge.

Long Position Occurs when an individual owns securities. An owner of 1000 shares of stock is said to be "Long the Stock."

Long Position (Options) An options position where a person has executed one or more options trades where the net result is that they are an "owner" or holder of options (i.e. the number of contracts bought exceeds the number of contracts sold).

Long Term Assets Value of property, equipment and other capital assets minus the depreciation. This is an entry in the bookkeeping records of a company, usually on a "cost" basis and thus does not necessarily reflect the market value of the assets.

Long Term Debt Value of obligations of over 1 year that require that interest be paid.

Long Term Debt/Capitalization Indicator of financial leverage. Shows long term debt as a proportion of the capital available. Determined by dividing long term debt by the sum of long term debt, preferred stock and common stockholders' equity.

Long Term Liabilities Amount owed for leases, bond repayment and other items due after 1 year.

Low Price The lowest (intraday) price of a stock over a certain period of time.

Management/Closely Held Shares Percentage of shares held by persons closely related to a company, as defined by the Securities and Exchange Commission. Part of these percentages often is included in Institutional Holdings--making the combined total of these percentages over 100. There is overlap as institutions sometimes acquire enough stock to be considered by the SEC to be closely allied to the company.

Margin Account (Stocks) A leverageable account in which stocks can be purchased for a combination of cash and a loan. The loan in the margin account is collateralized by the stock and, if the value of the stock drops sufficiently, the owner will be asked to either put in more cash, or sell a portion of the stock. Margin rules are federally regulated, but margin requirements and interest may vary among broker/dealers.

Margin Requirement (Options) The amount of cash an uncovered (naked) option writer is required to deposit and maintain to cover his daily position valuation and reasonably foreseeable intra- day price changes.

Market Capitalization The total dollar value of all outstanding shares. Computed as shares times current market price. It is a measure of corporate size.

Market Cycle The period between the 2 latest highs or lows of the S&P 500, showing net performance of a fund through both an up and a down market. A market cycle is complete when the S&P is 15 % below the highest point or 15 % above the lowest point (ending a down market). The dates of the last market cycle are: 12/04/87 to 10/11/90 (low to low).

Market Order An order to buy or sell a stock at the going price.

Minimum Purchases For mutual funds, the amount required to open a new account (Minimum Initial Purchase) or to deposit into an existing account (Minimum Additional Purchase). These minima may be lowered for buyers participating in an automatic purchase plan.

Money Market Fund A mutual fund that invests only in short term securities, such as bankers' acceptances, commercial paper, repurchase agreements and government bills. The net asset value per share is maintained at $1.00. Such funds are not federally insured, although the portfolio may consist of guaranteed securities and/or the fund may have private insurance protection.

Moving Average Used in charts and technical analysis, the average of security or commodity prices constructed in a period as short as a few days or as long as several years and showing trends for the latest interval. As each new variable is included in calculating the average, the last variable of the series is deleted.

Mutual Fund An open end investment company that pools investors' money to invest in a variety of stocks, bonds, or other securities. A mutual fund issues and redeems shares to meet demand, and the redemption value per share is the net asset value per share, less in some cases a redemption fee which represents a rear-end load. A closed end fund, often incorrectly called a mutual fund, is instead an investment trust. Both are investment companies regulated by the Investment Company Act of 1940.

National Association Of Securities Dealers (NASD) A self-regulatory organization with jurisdiction over certain broker-dealers. The NASD requires member brokers to register, and conducts examinations for compliance with net capital requirements and other regulations. It also conducts market surveillance of the over-the-counter (OTC) securities market. NASDAQ is a subsidiary of the NASD which facilitates the trading of approximately 5,000 of the most active OTC issues through an electronically connected network.

Net Asset Value (NAV) The value of a fund's investments. For a mutual fund, the net asset value per share usually represents the fund's market price, subject to a possible sales or redemption charge. For a closed end fund, the market price may vary significantly from the net asset value.

Net Income The company's total earnings, reflecting revenues adjusted for costs of doing business, depreciation, interest, taxes and other expenses.

Noise Price and volume fluctuations that can confuse interpretation of market direction.

No Load Mutual Fund An open-end investment company, shares of which are sold without a sales charge. There can be other distribution charges, however, such as Article 12b-1 fees. A true "no load" fund will have neither a sales charge nor a distribution fee.

NM Abbreviation for Not Meaningful.

Objective (Mutual Funds) The fund's investment strategy category as stated in the prospectus. There are more than 20 standardized categories.

Opening Purchase A transaction in which the purchaser's intention is to create or increase a long position in a given series of options.

Opening Sale A transaction in which the seller's intention is to create or increase a short position in a given series of options.

Open Interest The number of outstanding option contracts in the exchange market or in a particular class or series.

Option Gives the buyer the right, but not the obligation, to buy or sell stock at a set price on or before a given date. Investors, not companies, issue options. Investors who purchase call options bet the stock will be worth more than the price set by the option (the strike price), plus the price they paid for the option itself. Buyers of put options bet the stock's price will go down below the price set by the option.

Other Current Assets Value of non-cash assets, including prepaid expenses and accounts receivable, due within 1 year.

Other Long Term Liabilities Value of leases, future employee benefits, deferred taxes and other obligations not requiring interest payments that must be paid over a period of more than 1 year.

Other Sources Amount of funds generated during the period from operations by sources other than depreciation or deferred taxes. Part of Free Cash Flow calculation.

Out of the Money A call option is out-of-the-money if the strike price is greater than the market price of the underlying security. A put option is out-of-the-money if the strike price is less than the market price of the underlying security.

Overbought/Oversold Indicator An indicator that attempts to define when prices have moved too far and too fast in either direction and thus are vulnerable to reaction.

Payment Date Date on which a declared stock dividend or a bond interest payment is scheduled to be made.

Phone Switching In mutual funds, the ability to transfer shares between funds in the same family by telephone request. There may be a charge associated with these transfers. Phone switching is also possible among different fund families if the funds are held in street name by a participating broker/dealer.

Pivot Price level established as being significant by market's failure to penetrate or as being significant when a sudden increase in volume accompanies the move through the price level.

Point and Figure Chart A price-only chart that takes into account only whole integer changes in price, i.e., a 2-point change. Point and figure charting disregards the element of time and is solely used to record changes in price.

Preferred Stock A security that shows ownership in a corporation and gives the holder a claim, prior to the claim of common stockholders, on earnings and also generally on assets in the event of liquidation. Most preferred stock pays a fixed dividend, stated in a dollar amount or as a percentage of par value. This stock does not usually carry voting rights.

Premium The price of an option contract, determined on the exchange, which the buyer of the option pays to the option writer for the rights to the option contract.

Prices Price of a share of common stock on the date shown. Highs and lows are based on the highest and lowest intraday trading price.

Price/Book Ratio Compares a stock's market value to the value of total assets less total liabilities (book). Determined by dividing current price by common stockholders' equity per share (book value), adjusted for stock splits. Also called Market-to-Book.

Price/Earnings Ratio Shows the "multiple" of earnings at which a stock sells. Determined by dividing current price by current earnings per share (adjusted for stock splits). Earnings per share for the P/E ratio is determined by dividing earnings for past 12 months by the number of common shares outstanding. Higher "multiple" means investors have higher expectations for future growth, and have bid up the stock's price.

P/E Ratio Equation Assume XYZ Co sells for $25.50 per share and has earned $2.55 per share this year. $25.50 = 10 times $2.55
In this example, XYZ stock sells for 10 times earnings.

Price/Sales Ratio Determined by dividing stock's current price by revenue per share (adjusted for stock splits). Revenue per share for the P/S ratio is determined by dividing revenue for past 12 months by number of shares outstanding.

Primary Market The first buyer of a newly issued security buys that security in the primary market. All subsequent trading of those securities is done in the secondary market.

Profit Margin Indicator of profitability. Determined by dividing net income by revenue for the same 12-month period. Result is shown as a percentage.

Program Trading Trades based on signals from computer programs, usually entered directly from the trader's computer to the market's computer system and executed automatically.

Prospectus Formal written document to sell securities that describes the plan for a proposed business enterprise, or the facts concerning an existing one, that an investor needs to make an informed decision. Prospectuses are used by Mutual Funds to describe the fund objectives, risks and other essential information.

Proxy Document intended to provide shareholders with information necessary to vote in an informed manner on matters to be brought up at a stockholders' meeting. Includes information on closely held shares. Shareholders can and often do give management their proxy, representing the right and responsibility to vote their shares as specified in the proxy statement.

Put Option An option contract that gives the holder the right to sell (or "put"), and places upon the writer the obligation to purchase, a specified number of shares of the underlying stock at the given strike price on or before the expiration date of the contract.

Quick Ratio   Indicator of a company's financial strength (or weakness). Calculated by taking current assets less inventories, divided by current liabilities. Also called Acid Test.

Range   The difference between the high and low price during a given period.

Return   The percentage gain or loss for a mutual fund in a specific time period. This number assumes that all distributions are reinvested.

Record Date   Date by which a shareholder must officially own shares in order to be entitled to a dividend. For example, a firm might declare a dividend on Nov 1, payable Dec 1 to holders of record Nov 15. Once a trade is executed an investor becomes the "owner of record" on settlement, which currently takes 5 business days for securities, and one business day for mutual funds. Stocks trade ex-dividend the fourth day before the record date, since the seller will still be the owner of record and is thus entitled to the dividend.

Redemption Charge   The commission charged by a mutual fund when redeeming shares. For example, a 2 % redemption charge (also called a "back end load") on the sale of shares valued at $1000 will result in payment of $980 (or 98 % of the value) to the investor. This charge may decrease or be eliminated as shares are held for longer time periods.

Relative Strength   A stock's price movement over the past year as compared to a market index (the S&P 500). Value below 1.0 means the stock shows relative weakness in price movement (underperformed the market); a value above 1.0 means the stock shows relative strength over the 1-year period. Equation for Relative Strength: [current stock price/year-ago stock price] [current S&P 500/year-ago S&P 500] .

Retracement   A price movement in the opposite direction of the previous trend.

Return on Assets (ROA)   Indicator of profitability. Determined by dividing net income for the past 12 months by total assets. Result is shown as a percentage.

Return on Equity (ROE) Indicator of profitability. Determined by dividing net income for the past 12 months by common stockholders' equity (adjusted for stock splits). Result is shown as a percentage.

Reverse Stock Split A proportionate decrease in the number of shares, but not the value of shares of stock held by shareholders. Shareholders maintain the same percentage of equity as before the split. For example, a 1-for-3 split would result in stockholders owning 1 share for every 3 shares owned before the split. A firm generally institutes a reverse split to boost its stock's market price and attract investors.

Rights Offering Issuance of "rights" to current shareholders allowing them to purchase additional shares, usually at a discount to market price. Shareholders who do not exercise these rights are usually diluted by the offering. Rights are often transferrable, allowing the holder to sell them on the open market to others who may wish to exercise them. Rights offerings are particularly common to closed end funds, which cannot otherwise issue additional common stock.

Sales Charge The fee charged by a mutual fund when purchasing shares, usually payable as a commission to a marketing agent, such as a financial advisor, who is thus compensated for his assistance to a purchaser. It represents the difference, if any, between the share purchase price and the share net asset value.

SEC The Securities and Exchange Commission, the primary federal regulatory agency of the securities industry.

Secondary Market A market that provides for the purchase or sale of previously owned securities. Most trading is done in the secondary market. The New York Stock Exchange, as well as all other stock exchanges, the bond markets, etc., are secondary markets.

Selling Short If an investor thinks the price of a stock is going down, the investor could borrow the stock from a broker and sell it. Eventually, s/he must buy the stock back on the open market. For instance, you borrow 1000 shares of XYZ on July 1 and sell it for $8 per share. Then, on Aug 1, you purchase 1000 shares of XYZ at $7 per share. You've made $1000 (less commissions and other fees) by selling short.

Series Options: All option contracts of the same class that also have the same unit of trade, expiration date, and exercise price. Stocks: shares which have common characteristics, such as rights to ownership and voting, dividends, par value, etc. In the case of many foreign shares, one series may be owned only by citizens of the country in which the stock is registered.

Settlement Date The date on which payment is made to settle a trade. For stocks traded on US exchanges, settlement is currently 5 business days after the trade, but this will be reduced to 3 days in 1995. For mutual funds, settlement usually occurs in the U.S. the day following the trade. In some regional markets, foreign shares may require months to settle.

Shares Certificates or book entries representing ownership in a corporation or similar entity.

Share Repurchase Program by which a corporation buys back its own shares in the open market. It is usually done when shares are undervalued. Since it reduces the number of shares outstanding and thus increases earnings per share, it tends to elevate the market value of the remaining shares held by stockholders.

Short Position (Options) A position wherein a person's interest in a particular series of options is as a net writer (i.e., the number of contracts sold exceeds the number of contracts bought).

Short Position (Stocks) Occurs when a person sells stocks s/he does not yet own. Shares must be borrowed, before the sale, to make "good delivery" to the buyer. Eventually, the shares must be bought to close out the transaction. Technique is used when an investor believes the stock price is going down.

Short Sale Selling a security that the seller does not own but is committed to repurchasing eventually. It is used to capitalize on an expected decline in the security's price.

Slippage   The difference between estimated transaction costs and actual transaction costs. The difference is usually composed of revisions to price difference or spread and commission costs.

SIC   Abbreviation for Standard Industrial Classification. Each 4-digit code represents a unique business activity.

Stock Dividend   Payment of a corporate dividend in the form of stock rather than cash. The stock dividend may be additional shares in the company, or it may be shares in a subsidiary being spun off to shareholders. Stock dividends are often used to conserve cash needed to operate the business. Unlike a cash dividend, stock dividends are not taxed until sold.

Stop (-Loss) Order   An order to sell a stock when the price falls to a specified level.

Strike Price   The stated price per share for which underlying stock may be purchased (in the case of a call) or sold (in the case of a put) by the option holder upon exercise of the option contract.

10-K   Annual report required by the SEC each year. Provides a comprehensive overview of a company's state of business. Must be filed within 90 days after fiscal year end. A 10Q report is filed quarterly.

Tick Indicator   A market indicator based on the number of stocks whose last trade was an uptick or a downtick. Used as an indicator of market sentiment or psychology to try to predict the market's trend.

Time Value   The portion of the premium that is based on the amount of time remaining until the expiration date of the option contract, and that the underlying components that determine the value of the option may change during that time. Time value is generally equal to the difference between the premium and the intrinsic value.

Total Revenue   Total sales and other revenue for the period shown. Known as "turnover" in the UK.

Trade A verbal (or electronic) transaction involving one party buying a security from another party. Once a trade is consummated, it is considered "done" or final. Settlement occurs 1-5 business days later.

Trade Date The date on which a trade occurs. Trades generally settle (are paid for) 1-5 business days after a trade date. With stocks, settlement is generally 5 business days after the trade. TRADING RANGE The difference between the high and low prices traded during a period of time; with commodities, the high/low price limit established by the exchange for a specific commodity for any one day's trading.

Turnover Mutual Funds: A measure of trading activity during the previous year, expressed as a percentage of the average total assets of the fund. A turnover ratio of 25 % means that the value of trades represented one-fourth of the assets of the fund. Finance: The number of times a given asset, such as inventory, is replaced during the accounting period, usually a year. Corporate: The ratio of annual sales to net worth, representing the extent to which a company can growth without outside capital. Markets: The volume of shares traded as a percent of total shares listed during a specified period, usually a day or a year. Great Britain: Total revenue

12b-1 Fees The percent of a mutual fund's assets used to defray marketing and distribution expenses. The amount of the fee is stated in the fund's prospectus. The SEC has recently proposed that 12b1 fees in excess of 0.25% be classed as a load. A true "no load" fund has neither a sales charge nor 12b1 fee.

Type The classification of an option contract as either a put or a call.

Uncovered Call A short call option position in which the writer does not own shares of underlying stock represented by his option contracts. Also called a "naked" call, it is much riskier for the writer than a covered call, where the writer owns the underlying stock. If the buyer of a call exercises the option to call, the writer would be forced to buy the stock at market price.

Uncovered Put A short put option position in which the writer does not have a corresponding short stock position or has not deposited, in a cash account, cash or cash equivalents equal to the exercise value of the put. Also called "naked" puts, the writer has pledged to buy the stock at a certain price if the buyer of the options chooses to exercise it. The nature of uncovered options means the writer's risk is unlimited.

Underlying Security Options: the security subject to being purchased or sold upon exercise of an option contract. For example, IBM stock is the underlying security to IBM options. Depositary receipts: The class, series and number of the foreign shares represented by the depositary receipt.

Volatility A measure of risk based on standard deviation in fund performance over 3 years. Scale is 1-9; higher rating indicates higher risk.

Std Deviation	Rating	Std Deviation	Rating
up to 7.99	1	20.00-22.99	6
8.00-10.99	2	23.00-25.99	7
11.00-13.99	3	26.00-28.99	8
14.00-16.99	4	29.00 and up	9
17.00-19.99	5		

Wallflower Stock that has fallen out of favor with investors; tends to have a low P/E.

Wanted For Cash A statement displayed on market tickers which indicates that a bidder will pay cash for same day settlement of a block of a specified security.

Warrant A security entitling the holder to buy a proportionate amount of stock at some specified future date at a specified price, usually one higher than current market. This "warrant" is then traded as a security, the price of which reflects the value of the underlying stock. Warrants are usually issued as a "sweetener" bundled with another class of security to enhance the marketability of the latter,

Wasting Asset An asset which has a limited life and thus, decreases in value (depreciates) over time. Also applied to consumed assets, such as gas, and termed "depletion."

Watch List A list of securities selected for special surveillance by a brokerage, exchange or regulatory organization; firms on the list are often takeover targets, companies planning to issue new securities or stocks showing unusual activity.

Withdrawal Plan The ability to establish automatic periodic mutual fund redemptions and have proceeds mailed directly to the investor.

Writer The seller of an option contract.

W-Type Bottom A double bottom where the price or indicator chart has the appearance of a W.

Yield The percentage rate of return paid on a stock in the form of dividends, or the rate of interest paid on a bond or note.

Yield to Call The percentage rate of a bond or note, if your were to buy and hold the security until the call date. This yield is valid only if the security is called prior to maturity. Generally bonds are callable over several years and normally are called at a slight premium. The calculation of yield to call is based on the coupon rate, length of time to the call and the market price.

Yield to Maturity (YTM) The percentage rate of return paid on a bond, note or other fixed income security if you buy and hold it to its maturity date. The calculation for YTM is based on the coupon rate, length of time to maturity and market price. It assumes that coupon interest paid over the life of the bond will be reinvested at the same rate.

Index